PATTERNS

PATTERNS

WAYS TO DEVELOP A GOD-FILLED LIFE

MEL LAWRENZ

GRAND RAPIDS, MICHIGAN 49530 USA

ZONDERVAN™

Patterns

Copyright © 2003 by Mel Lawrenz

Requests for information should be addressed to:

Zondervan, *Grand Rapids, Michigan 49530*

Library of Congress Cataloging-in-Publication Data

Lawrenz, Mel.
  Patterns : ways to develop a God-filled life / Mel Lawrenz.
    p. cm.
  ISBN 0-310-24810-8
  1. Christian life. I. Title.
  BV4501.3 .L395 2003
  248.4—dc21
                                                           2002156681

This edition printed on acid-free paper.

Published in association with the literary agency of Alive Communications, Inc., 7680 Goddard Street, Suite 200, Colorado Springs, CO 80920.

Interior design by Beth Shagene

Printed in the United States of America

---

03 04 05 06 07 08 09 /❖ DC/ 10 9 8 7 6 5 4 3 2 1

To Ingrid,

my wife, whom I love
and who shows me
grace and truth every day

CONTENTS

PREFACE

One weekend I somewhat spontaneously offered to write and send, via email, a weekly essay on spiritual growth to anyone at Elmbrook Church who was interested. That weekend seven hundred addresses were turned in on scraps of paper, business cards, and offering envelopes. Over the next few months the list grew to two thousand, then three thousand, addresses from over thirty different countries. Some people told me they were forwarding the essays to dozens of other people. This book is a revised and expanded collection of those essays.

It is obvious that people today are longing for deeper spiritual growth. To put it another way, we're all looking for how to live a God-filled life.

The premise of this book is simply this: spiritual life and health is a matter of how God shapes the contours of our character, both by his direct influence and by the gradual, faithful, progressive practices of good spiritual habits or disciplines. The Bible talks about such contours and habits as patterns. This book is mainly a study of the fruit of the Spirit (Galatians 5) as "character patterns" and of basic spiritual habits or disciplines as "devotion patterns."

Having been a pastor for twenty-two years and having had the opportunity to talk to many people about their spiritual lives, I am very aware that we need encouragement in the forms of both prodding and comfort. God surely does not want us stuck in spiritual defeatism, but neither should we get overly self-confident and platitudinous about living a godly life.

I take comfort in the fact that God gives us a new start each day and shows us the small steps that need to be taken each hour to follow him, the one who is always drawing us toward himself.

PART ONE

MORE THAN ADVENTURE

IN SEARCH OF THE FULL LIFE

He stood on the deck of the *Pilar* and scanned the Caribbean swells off the coast of Cuba for the telltale sign of a periscope or water breaking over the steel skin of a German U-boat. Not many men would purposely equip their fishing boats with bazookas, grenades, and a couple of .50-caliber machine guns in the hope of confronting enemy submarines, but that's the kind of man he was. His scheme was this: lure in a U-boat to a distance of about fifty yards, wait for an enemy boarding party to emerge onto the deck of the submarine, then rev up the motors, close the gap, begin shooting, and lob grenades down the conning tower. It was a different kind of sport than the marlin fishing that had attracted him to the tropics. But Ernest Hemingway was never satiated by any adventure he undertook. By all accounts he packed ten lives into one.

Hemingway was a promising young newspaperman before being wounded in Italy in World War I, and while still in his twenties, he began writing novels like *The Sun Also Rises* and *A Farewell to Arms*. Bullfighting, big game hunting, deep-sea fishing, and war were his passions. He made sure he got close to the action in World

War II, landing with the American troops at Normandy as a newsman. He was fully engaged in the most important happenings of his time. He lived in Spain, Paris, Key West, Cuba, and Idaho. He survived exploding shells in his hotel room, getting hit by a taxi, and a plane crash in Africa.

Yet for all the fullness of his life, Hemingway experienced life as an empty hole and fought a losing battle with dread and anxiety—the sad payoff of his hedonistic obsessions. His heavy drinking was pure escape and pure abuse. He went through four marriages. He moved in and out of severe depression and was twice hospitalized to receive electroshock treatments. In the end, this Nobel Prize– and Pulitzer Prize–winning novelist put a shotgun to his head and ended his life. How can it be that a life that appeared so full could be so empty?

"MY LIFE IS COMPLETELY EMPTY"

I've heard it many times over the years, but my heart still sinks when I hear someone say, "My life is completely empty." It's a significant plea, one that always makes me stop and think: What is it that I really long for in my life? What will prevent my life from just emptying out before my eyes? And this phrase comes to mind: I want to—I need to—live a God-filled life.

When I'm honest, I admit that there are so many other competing desires in my life, so many other internal voices, that my longing for a God-filled life is easily compromised by my own self-centeredness and by the clamor of living in this world. I know I need to find ways every day to think about and follow patterns that will keep me in touch with this one unalterable reality: God "fills everything in every way" (Eph. 1:23).

And he is the only one who can.

The opposite of a filled life is an empty life. Yet for everything that seems to offer a certain fullness of life—our work, our recreation, our relationships, our belongings, our adventures—there is only one who can really fill our lives, or fulfill our lives.

Who can put in our hearts a deep and enduring sense of peace? Who can motivate us to truly love? Who can fill our minds with thoughts that will elevate us and make us wiser people? Who can guide our wills so that the decisions we make will be smart and respectable? Who can give us a sense of greatness and nobility in our lives? Who can fill us with strength when we're in the middle of a struggle? Only God.

FILLED, BUT WITH WHAT?

There's filling, and then there's filling. My days fill up easily enough, but fullness is something different. It is a kind of filling that happens at a deeply spiritual level.

Do you know that moment when you're waking up and you first realize what day it is? Perhaps your mind begins to lay out the activities of the day as you're still blinking and yawning. Lately I've been struck how as I contemplate the day ahead, I have had a strange sense that the day has been spent already. It's Wednesday, so that means study time in the morning (but I know that time will fly by), lunch meeting at noon, worship meeting in the early afternoon, appointments for the rest of the afternoon, and probably more paper on my desk at the end of the day than at the start. The sense of crowding also has a lot to do with the fact that my children are now sixteen and fourteen, and their schedules are getting fuller all the time; my wife and I have more interests and more personal contacts than ever before; I've got more professional responsibilities than I could have dreamed of; and I get about forty-eight hours of ideas for every twenty-four hours I'm allotted.

Now I know I would live in dismay over this except for a word a friend gave me years ago, a wonderfully leveling truth: God has given me, and everyone else, twenty-four hours a day—no more, no less. Yet at the start of the day I still hear this irritating voice telling me, "The day is already spent, and you haven't gotten everything *done*."

We all know how easily a day can get filled up, but the question is, Will it be filled with what is good? Will it be filled by God?

WHAT DOES IT MEAN TO BE GOD-FILLED?

There are a few simple things we can do today to make sure we open our eyes to God's presence: praying at moments scattered throughout the day, reading from the Bible, getting out in the fresh air to walk and meditate on issues that will make a difference not just for today but for many days to come. But it's not up to us to insert God into our days. It is not that we take some God-filled container and pour God into our day. It doesn't work that way, because God is not that kind of God. Living a God-filled life does not mean scheduling God for an appointment or two and feeling satisfied that we did God the favor of squeezing him into a very busy schedule.

No, living a God-filled life is a great mystery and the greatest adventure any of us can take up. It all begins with this reality: God "fills everything in every way." That means that God created everything, he is present everywhere, always, and he is the unrivaled master of the universe. Psalm 24:1 (KJV) says: "the earth is the LORD's and the fullness thereof." Since I live my life on this earth, I know that his fullness must be all around me: beneath me, above me, beside me, and in me. It is not up to me to fill my life with God; rather, I need God to open my life, by faith, to his fullness, which comes through Christ. How this happens involves a lifetime of lessons and a training of spiritual vision so we see both God's large and subtle movements. And always the filling comes as a direct work of the Spirit of God.

When I think about this I immediately know what a child I am. My thoughts and conversations so easily stay in the shallows of concerns for my food and clothing, schedules and entertainments, aches and pleasures. It is not hard for me to ignore God. My dinner and my friendships are so much easier to manage, and they make no demands for my allegiance. It is easier to put on a neatly pressed shirt and pants than it is to straighten out my attitude. Talking to my wife is in many ways easier than praying to God; I don't need much faith when the person I'm talking to is standing there in the kitchen with me.

And yet—to ignore God for long requires a heart made of stone. There are those questions not answered by television, newspaper, or a family member. God puts out a spiritual beacon of sorts which attracts us like bugs to a porch light. Going without worshiping is like not seeing the sun for days on end. Not talking about God is like being locked in a room of stale and spent air.

The Bible says that "from the fullness of [Christ's] grace we have all received one blessing after another" (John 1:16), and that is because Jesus "came from the Father, full of grace and truth" (1:14). Now stop and think about that. Aren't these two spiritual qualities— grace and truth—a complete summary of all we could hope to possess? I have often said that I could hope for nothing more in my marriage than that it be full of grace and truth. My kids? I pray that they will come to adulthood with a trained instinct to love and to live in reality. I think about the church I serve. Is there anything more I could hope for than that people find in that community a treasury of grace and truth?

Here is John's point. We receive "one blessing after another" because of the fullness of Christ which fills the lives of those who attach themselves to him. If you or I had walked with Jesus, we would have seen one act of mercy after another absolutely integrated with one pronouncement of truth after another. He excoriated the Pharisees but met with one of them, a seeker, under the cloak of darkness. He graced the woman at the well with his patient words, and also confronted her immoral pattern of life. And when we speak with Jesus we can count on this: his mercy will flow toward us, and he will expose every sin we try to hide from him.

God's greatest desire for us, the good plan of a loving Father, is that we "become mature, attaining to the whole measure of the fullness of Christ" (Eph. 4:13). Here is a pile of words that speak of fullness. *Mature* means complete, lacking nothing. *Whole measure* indicates being full to capacity. *Fullness of Christ* means that God wants to fill our lives with the very character of the Lord and a continual consciousness of his presence.

Jesus has all the fullness of God dwelling in him (Col. 1:19), and consequently, if our lives are connected with Jesus, we have fullness in Christ: "For in Christ all the fullness of the Deity lives in bodily form, and you have been given fullness in Christ, who is the head over every power and authority" (Col. 2:9–10). John Calvin wrote of this passage: "'You are made full' does not mean that the perfection of Christ is transfused into us, but that there are in him resources from which we may be filled, that nothing be wanting in us."

What you and I need to do each day is not just fill up our time and empty out our energy, falling into bed at night merely spent. A full life comes from having the gateways to mind, heart, and soul open to the person and work of Jesus.

BEYOND ADVENTURE

The fullness of Christ is all about the most significant longing any of us can have—a yearning not merely for adventure but for much more than adventure. It is about God's longing for us. He looks at us, knows what he created us for, knows what we are capable of. God wants us to have fullness in our lives, and he brings it about not by filling our schedules but by filling us. But with what does he fill us? The biblical answer, loud and clear, is love. Somehow when God's love is able to flow into our consciousness and experience, it is translated into the muscle tissue of character. And should that surprise us? Are we hungrier for anything more than love?

Listen to the yearning in the words of the apostle Paul as he prayed for fellow believers: "And I pray that you, being rooted and established in love, may have power, together with all the saints, to grasp how wide and long and high and deep is the love of Christ, and to know this love that surpasses knowledge—that you may be filled to the measure of all the fullness of God" (Eph. 3: 17–19). We need to have the power to grasp the knowledge of the love of Christ, to really own it—to know how wide it is (reaching all around the world), how long it is (stretching from eternity past to eternity future), how high it is (elevating us to the qualities of heaven) and how deep it is (penetrating down to the darkest pits of our lives).

Our lives may be filled with activity (whether important or trivial, urgent or casual) and with people (from those in our inner orbit to the crowds we just bump into along the way), but fullness has to happen within. A person can go on safaris, hunt U-boats, and meet heads of state and still have an empty heart. Now is the time to do something about our emptiness, not when emptiness leads to desperation and hopelessness. The fullness of Christ is available, but it must be "grasped," and to do that we need "power." Any one of us can take Paul's prayer and make it our own.

PRAY THIS

Lord, I pray that I would have roots as strong as those of a magnificent tree, going deeply into your love, and as strong as a building built on the foundation of your love. Please give me the ability to take in, to understand, to apply, and to own the reality of your love, which is wide enough to get around my whole life, long enough to last my whole life and beyond, high enough to elevate me to the stature you desire, and deep enough to fill the unseen pockets of decay and emptiness in the hidden parts of my life. Please fill my life and fulfill my life because I know—I know—I cannot do it on my own. Amen.

It takes a lifetime to begin to grasp the reality of these truths, but we don't need to wait our whole lives. On any given day we can open ourselves to the fullness of Christ and live a God-filled day. And when we live one God-filled day after another, we will enjoy (by God's gift alone!) a God-filled life.

Now there are things that we can do that will open our lives to this fullness of God. And that is the purpose of this book. When we have a sustained commitment to certain spiritually rich patterns in our lives, we will be exposed repeatedly to the grace and truth of Christ, and we will be profoundly shaped by them.

FOR PERSONAL REFLECTION

1. Think of a typical day or week in your life. When are you most aware of God, and when are you least aware of him?

2. Complete this sentence: I need God to fill my life in these ways … (For example, "I need God to help me not be so fearful.")

3. What circumstances in life tend to empty or drain you? (For example, a degrading work environment.)

4. Think about someone you know who has a vivid sense of God's presence and activity day by day. What do you think he or she is doing that promotes an awareness of the fullness of Christ?

5. What is the difference between just talking about God and really living a God-filled life?

6. If one way of looking at the fullness of Christ is that he was "full of grace and truth," come up with some specific examples of where he demonstrated grace (love, mercy, generosity) and truth (living authentically and explaining reality to people). (For example, the feeding of the five thousand was an act of grace because Christ knew the people were hungry, and it was an act of truth because he taught that he was the bread sent from heaven.)

LIVING BY PATTERN

It was twelve years ago, but I still remember how nervous I was as my wife and I sat at the heavy walnut table in the office of the home builder. The lady on the other side of the table removed the rubber band from the rolled-up architectural drawings, which she then rolled out flat on the table. They still smelled of the chemicals used in the process of making blueprints and felt cool to the touch. And there it was: a two-dimensional drawing of the home we were going to build. On successive pages were different views of the house, perfectly drawn. Were we really going to do this? Were we in over our heads? Would we really raise our kids in this home that was just lines on paper, an idea in the head of a designer?

In the weeks that followed I went time and again to the site where our home was being built and saw one subcontractor after another arrive with that same set of blueprints bearing our signatures. Whether it was a carpenter, a mason, an electrician, a plumber, or anyone else, they simply looked at that plan—that pattern—and did what it told them to do, exactly where it told them to do it. And when our home was completed after eight weeks, every wall, every counter, every door, and every electrical outlet was placed exactly where the plan said it should be. An idea had become a reality.

Planets, DNA, and Habits

All of life is built on patterns. In the natural world bees form their honeycombs, robins piece together their nests, trees add ring upon ring, geese migrate north and then south, planets loop around the sun, all in progressive and wonderfully consistent patterns. Some patterns seem to be purely the joyful expression of the exuberant Creator: the waves of sand in the desert, the waves of water in the ocean, the orderly and vivacious bands of color of the rainbow.

There are many patterns in human life, like the microscopic strings of DNA, a different kind of blueprint, which determined whether your hair color would be auburn or black, whether your height would be five feet or six, whether your nose would be slightly crooked to the left or to the right, and whether your cholesterol level would be 180 or 300. Mathematics is built on paterns. An algorithm is a systematic procedure for solving a problem in a finite number of steps. With the whir and click of a computer hard drive, a pattern of data is collected, sorted, and processed, all as a matrix of 0s and 1s, but capable of carrying a Shakespeare play or a digital image of a far-away galaxy.

And then there are chosen patterns, the behaviors that shape our character, form our reputation, and determine our satisfaction in life. These are our habits. How many hours do you sleep at night? Do you smoke cigarettes throughout the day? Do you pray? How do you speak to your parents, to your spouse, and to your kids? How do you respond to stressful circumstances? What do you do when you feel angry? What do you read? What are you expecting to happen when you go to church?

This list could go on and on, because anything we do in life with any kind of repetition is a life pattern—whether it builds us up or tears us down. And there's the rub: a good pattern progressively builds us up, but a bad pattern relentlessly erodes our humanity, like ocean waves pounding a coast. Being unaware of our life patterns is about the biggest gamble any of us can take.

In this book we will first consider the character patterns of a God-filled life, the patterns of love, joy, peace, patience, kindness, goodness, faithfulness, gentleness, and self-control. Then we'll look at devotion patterns, acts that draw us closer to God, such as praying, reading spiritually, and worshiping.

How are these two types of patterns related? From one perspective, devotion patterns are the things we *do* so that we can *be* people with good character patterns. But this is not a simple formula. Our life with God can't be broken down neatly into techniques or methods leading to results. There's more mystery to it than that. It is oftentimes true that a character trait develops after the training of spiritual discipline, like joy coming from a regular habit of worship and prayer. Then again, sometimes God just lays a treasury of love in a person's heart, and character takes a leap forward in the discovery. At other times it is a crisis that precipitates a change in character. I've known more than one husband and father, for instance, who suffered a serious heart attack in midlife and gained a conspicuous degree of faithfulness and gentleness as a result.

Along the way we will consider relationship patterns that are highly influential in the formation of character, because some people reinforce in us good characteristics and habits and some people pull us down. And we also need to look at patterns that are personally destructive, call them "antipatterns" if you will, because instead of pulling our lives together, they smash them apart.

DESIGN, ORDER, AND CONSISTENCY

I am enthused about the concept of patterning because it assures me that if, with God's help, we choose and practice good life patterns, certain qualities will be built into our lives.

First, good life patterns will create a *design* for our lives. Every person's life has a certain shape or form. Spiritual health and strength are not random but are the progressive building of a sound mind, of proportional emotions, and of a trained will. But who can figure out what this looks like? God designed the blueprint for spiritual health and strength, and he takes our misshapen selves and forms us according to the image of Christ. The qualities known as the fruit of the Spirit comprise the finely designed blueprint of what human character should be. And when we commit to habits like prayer and worship, we are putting ourselves in God's workshop, not always knowing what the work of the day will be but assured that God keeps crafting according to a design in his mind.

Second, good life patterns will create *order* in our lives. Someone smarter than us needs to help us figure out how all the roles and functions of our lives can work harmoniously and authentically. On any given day I've got to be a husband, a father, a pastor, a neighbor, a friend. I've got to take care of a house, a family, a church. I may need to repair a broken door, mend a relationship, balance an out-of-whack checkbook. I need to know what to keep, what to give away, what to throw away, what to let into my house and life. I need order!

So this is what God does. He assures us first of all that we don't need to feel hopelessly overwhelmed by all the options and responsibilities in life. Character and devotion (as defined by God) combine to provide order for the day. I know I must begin the day with some quiet moments with God. Praying sorts out what is really important, and reading Scripture is like looking at a compass, giving me order and a sense of direction. I know that as a family we need to start the day on the right foot by greeting each other with kindness and to send everybody out the door with a sense of peace and love. I need to try to enter my work for the day with faithfulness to my responsibilities and self-control when it comes to my work habits. And at the end of the day, when the whole family is a bit worn out, patience will help us get along when frustrations or conflicts come up. Order is not just about organization. It is about spiritual direction.

Third, good life patterns will create *consistency* in our lives. We can't live by changing the moral rules of life as we move from one season of life to the next. Tuesday and Thursday may be very different days in my life, but I can't change my priorities every day of the week. Consistency is what we're looking for when we try to find a "normal" life. The alternative is chaos, which some people accept because they can't imagine life being any other way. But there is something better than shooting across the landscape like a tornado, tossing bits and scraps of life into the air.

If we go to worship only when we feel like it, we will miss out on the consistency of this rhythm. If we pray only on days when it is convenient or when we feel "spiritual," we will miss out on the cumulative effect of a continual dialogue with God. Patterning is a focused commitment to making a few habits and character traits the normal, the daily, the consistent. All good adventures are disciplined. Chaos brings more danger than life.

PATTERNING IN THE BIBLE

The idea of patterning appears in the Bible from beginning to end.

On Mount Sinai God gave Moses many specific instructions about what he wanted Moses to do. One set of instructions was a blueprint for building a kind of traveling worship center, the tabernacle. God gave Moses specific designs (for a tent, a table, a lampstand, an altar, an ark), the materials to be used (gold, silver, animal skins, acacia wood), and instructions on how this worship center would function. God had a plan, and he insisted that it be followed: "See that you make [these things] according to the *pattern* shown you on the mountain" (Ex. 25:40, emphasis added). Four times in the Old Testament and twice in the New (Acts 7:44; Heb. 8:5), it is stated that this place of meeting with God, designed by God as a spiritual masterpiece, was built exactly according to pattern.

Design. Order. Consistency.

Patterning is a vivid theme in the New Testament as well. This captivating word—meaning "pattern, type, likeness, copy, model, impression"—appears more than a dozen times and points to experiences and people that give definition to life. In Romans 5:14 Adam is called "a pattern of the one to come," that is, Jesus Christ. In other words, Adam as the original, perfect man and Jesus as the unalterable perfect man are patterns of how we are supposed to be. (Although Adam became a sort of antipattern.)

The apostle Paul urged people to model their lives on the good patterns of other believers ("Take note of those who live according to the pattern we gave you," Phil. 3:17; also 1 Tim. 1:7; 2 Thess. 3:9; Titus 2:7; 1 Peter 5:3). He warned against following the antipatterns found in this world ("Do not conform any longer to the pattern of this world, but be transformed," Rom. 12:2) and urged people to follow patterns of truth ("What you heard from me, keep as the pattern of sound teaching, with faith and love in Christ Jesus," 2 Tim. 1:13; compare Rom. 6:17).

The idea of patterning is that if we follow the designs God has described in great detail, if we follow those blueprints and keep steady in those rhythms, we will experience life with a fullness and soundness that comes only from God—just like building a home according to the plan of a master architect. Our lives can even become patterns for others to follow.

Are you willing to pray a prayer like this?

PRAY THIS

Dear Lord, I need your help! When I forget about you, my life is like a reed in the wind, blown this way and that by the many pressures and passions in me and in this world. I need you as the builder of my life. I need you to put together the pieces of my life according to the design that only you know, so that I will be built up into a person who is sound and good. Show me the parts and show me the whole. Help me to follow your plan. Amen.

FOR PERSONAL REFLECTION

1. What are the most influential habits (good or bad) in your life right now?

2. What are two patterns that you know you need to develop right now?

3. Who do you respect for having design, order, and consistency in their lives that you can observe and imitate?

4. Describe a situation in which one person's life was a model and an inspiration to someone else.

5. What specific instructions for life (particularly, instructions found in the Bible) do you believe are most important for you to focus on?

6. Sometimes God's designs for our lives come as a surprise or revelation. Have you had such an eye-opening experience, and if so, what was it?

PART TWO

CHARACTER PATTERNS

IF YOU WERE INVISIBLE

There is a story of a shepherd named Gyges who found a magic gold ring that had the power to make him invisible. He discovered its power quite by accident when he was sitting with some fellow shepherds and happened to twist the ring so that its bezel was on the inside of his hand. Twisting the ring back again, Gyges reappeared. Then human nature took over. Gyges realized that with this power he could go anywhere and do anything, so he moved into the royal court, seduced the queen, attacked and murdered the king, and took over the throne.

When Plato the Greek philosopher wrote of this fable in *The Republic,* he was making a simple point: we would quickly discover the true character of a person if that person had the power to be invisible. We find out what kind of people we are, in other words, by noticing how we behave when no one else can see us.

THE STAMP OF CHARACTER

The word *character* originates from a word for a stamp that leaves an imprint, like a die used to make coins. Your character is the very shape of your inner life (your thoughts, motives, values, impulses, responses), which is revealed in the shape of your outer life (your actions, behaviors, speech, relationships). And then this sobering thought: the shape of your character may be stamped on someone else's character, for good or for ill. Is character an important issue for public leaders, athletic heroes, and parents? How can it not be?

Your character is never defined by one or two significant righteous deeds or by one or two failings. The *pattern* of your life constitutes your character, the shape or the imprint of your life.

It's ironic that one's character is often revealed at one's funeral (when the person really is invisible!). Now I've officiated at enough funerals to know that people tend to polish the halo of the deceased, and perhaps that's a natural way of giving the deceased the benefit of the doubt (especially when his last chance is up). But in and through all the conversations, eulogies, and sympathy cards, the person's character is unveiled and the form, the shape, of a life is revealed.

THE FRUIT OF THE SPIRIT

What does good character look like? Here is a fine list of character qualities for any person living anywhere in the world at any time: love, joy, peace, patience, kindness, goodness, gentleness, faithfulness, self-control. These are what the Bible calls "the fruit of the Spirit" (Gal. 5:22–23), and they describe a Christlike life.

I remember a moment years ago when a troubled husband and wife sat in my office and poured out the frustrations and bitterness of their marriage. They couldn't say what they were hoping their marriage would be, but it certainly wasn't this! So I asked them: "How would you feel differently about your marriage today if you could use these kinds of words to describe it: love, joy, peace, patience, kindness, goodness, gentleness, faithfulness, self-control?" They seemed almost stunned, and in a hushed voice the wife said: "If we had those things, there's nothing else we would ask for." I told them that these were the qualities the Bible calls "the fruit of the Spirit," (I had an inkling these were brand-new ideas to them), and that "fruit" meant the final result, the spectacular gift, that comes from the presence of God's Spirit in our lives.

There are many ways to describe Christlikeness. (A superb description comes from the Gospel of John, which says Jesus was full of grace and truth.) But I wonder, if any of us had spent a month with Jesus, or a week, or even a day, might we not say that we had witnessed in his character love, joy, peace, patience, kindness, goodness, gentleness, faithfulness, and self-control?

In this section of the book we will take each of these qualities, each one a treasure, and ask, What does this quality look like when displayed in a person's life? And how can this quality be formed in my character?

WHAT WILL THEY SAY AT YOUR FUNERAL?

Do you want to be known as a patient person, a faithful and kind person? Do you want to enjoy a kind of peace that is like a deep-flowing, cool river? Do you sense that it is long past time to get some real self-control in your life? These are all wonderful qualities, the stuff of real character. But they are not achieved by performing occasional heroic acts. At your funeral your son or daughter is not likely to say, "Yes, I remember that one day when Mom was patient, that day when we broke *two* windows playing baseball. It was such a wonderful day! Too bad she was the picture of impatience every other day." None of us wants to be known as a person who is kind once every other month. We should all know that it's not good enough if people think we are loving and good because of the image we project and the public posture we take, when in reality we are empty inside. We may fool some of the people some of the time, but that is not an accomplishment of character. In an age when image is everything and some have even come to think that image is the only reality, we are more desperately in need of character than ever before.

The American revolutionary John Adams sometimes seems eclipsed by his brilliant contemporary Thomas Jefferson. Jefferson's face is carved in a sixty-foot section of granite on Mount Rushmore, after all, not Adams'. But how remarkable was the character of

Adams, a man for whom being second president of the United States was just one more vocation in a string of vocations serving the public, just one step in the journey of a lifetime. He sacrificed the comforts of home for months and years on end to live in Philadelphia and frame a new nation and to sojourn as an ambassador in the very alien country of the French. Adams longed to make a truly important contribution to society, but he was not allured by the vanities of public attention. He endured ostracism. He persevered in debating—word by word—the important documents of the revolution. Months of work were not too much to make sure the work was done precisely. Any accolades and gains in reputation had to be the natural outworking of honorable work. And at the end of a long life, Adams was able to reflect more on God and was filled with awe and appreciation even as the loved ones in his life passed away. Incredibly, Adams died on the Fourth of July, the exact day of the fiftieth anniversary of the Declaration of Independence of which he was the driving force. His dying words were not about himself but were instead "Jefferson still lives." Adams did not know that hours earlier, that same day, Thomas Jefferson had died many miles away.

Character is built over a lifetime.

ANYTHING WORTH BUILDING TAKES MANY FAITHFUL STEPS

How is character formed?

There is a traditional saying that goes like this: "Sow a thought, reap an action; sow an action, reap a habit; sow a habit, reap a character; sow a character, reap a destiny." In other words, character traits are built over a long period of time by the sustained repetition of right instincts and their matching acts. Character is built by the progressive patterning of a person's life.

But how do you gain patience as a character trait, for instance? How does it progress from thought to action to habit to character to destiny?

Joe knew that he was a fundamentally impatient person. He was used to getting what he wanted, when he wanted it. The problem was that as an adult living in the real world, Joe wasn't getting things his way like he used to as a kid. It wasn't that Joe had bad values and wanted the wrong things in life; he just didn't know how to wait for what he wanted. As Joe grew in faith, however, he learned about the patience of God. He learned too about the patience of faith giants like Abraham, Moses, and Paul—men who went to their graves not fully realizing the work of their lives. After all, the only real estate in the Promised Land that Abraham owned at his death was the grave in which he was laid. Joe realized that his impatience was the cause of many conflicts in his life and tensions in his home.

Joe's prayer, worship, and reading of Scripture became a search for a new paradigm of living. He asked God just to help him gain a more relaxed attitude toward life. Gradually, this new attitude took root. Joe's habits changed so that he began to live life instead of attacking it. His expectations of his kids and wife became more relaxed. He gave up the notion that he knew how many decades he would live and that he knew the perfect script for his life. In short, Joe gained back his life. His family relationships and friendships developed deeper roots. And as a bonus, Joe slept better and had more energy.

Character traits develop over long periods of time and through sustained commitment. Is that bad news or good news? I think it's tremendous news. Don't be disheartened that you can't just decide to wake up tomorrow morning and have a completely reformed character. Instead, be encouraged that the building of character can begin at any moment. Anything worth building takes many faithful steps. And the moment the steps begin, character begins to take shape. For instance, the genesis of real peace for many people begins when they take the step to really admit to God the things they think they need to hide from him—as if anyone could. One step, but what a giant leap!

Be even more encouraged that God is there to put his unlimited energy into the formation of our character. Here is how he does it. Jesus, as the Son of God, is "the radiance of God's glory and the exact representation [literally, "character"] of his being, sustaining all things by his powerful word" (Heb. 1:3). In other words, just as a die is used to stamp a coin and every tiny engraved detail on the die is exactly reproduced on the coin, so it is with Jesus and God the Father.

THE CHARACTER OF JESUS

Jesus is the perfect pattern of God's own character. He is the same character, the exact stamp of God's character, whether he is visible or invisible.

And this Jesus is the Word of God—God's whispers and God's shouts, his consolation and his confrontation. God has spoken to us, and everyday he is still speaking to us, clearly, consistently, repetitively, faithfully, fully, patiently, lovingly. In the life of Jesus the stamp of God's character was impressed on the world. Jesus is the perfect God, and Jesus is the perfect man. Every time we talk to Jesus we expose our claylike nature to his impress—when we see Christ with us in our homes, offices, parks, or malls; when we realize that Jesus is there with us even when we are getting lured into an argument or are tempted to open a lewd magazine; and certainly when we think of Christ in the sanctuary as we sing his praise and in the quiet rooms where we pray. In every place and in every way Christ is there for one purpose: to transform our impressionable minds and hearts into the shape that God will call once again "very good!"

It may be true that we learn something about our character when no one else can see us. But here is another way to look at it: when no one else can see us, *only* God sees us. And it takes a huge step of humility, faith, and courage to say, "Okay God, what do you see?"

PRACTICE THIS

1. Make a mental note every time you see someone displaying a quality of good character (even someone in a movie, book, or TV show). What, in a word, is that respectable character quality? And why did you notice it?
2. Say at least a sentence prayer in every room or space you linger in during this week. In other words, make yourself con-

sciously aware of the presence of Christ in every spot you occupy day by day, and notice how you look at your life differently. What difference does it make in your life when you envision Jesus right there in the room with you?

FOR PERSONAL REFLECTION

1. Try to think of one person whom you look up to as a person of real character (someone you know directly or indirectly). Why do you think this person has good character? What do you think that person has done in his or her life to develop those patterns?

2. What are two or three character qualities you think you need to grow in?

3. Read Hebrews 1:1–3 several times and in different translations if possible. What aspects of the character of Christ have made the deepest impression on you?

THE MOST EXCELLENT WAY

Love

Our eighth-grade Sunday school class met in a basement room with a black-and-white tiled floor. We sat on tan-colored folding metal chairs in neat rows, facing the middle-aged teacher with curly gray hair who alternated between sitting and standing in front of the twenty of us. I don't remember any specific thing we learned, and I don't know that I should, since we generally acquire truth after many voices have said the same thing. But I do remember two things. I was deeply impressed by the meticulous and slow reverence with which our teacher read from and commented on the small paperback paraphrase of the New Testament, which was our only textbook for the class. And I also remember something this man said at the end of every class. He looked straight at us and said deliberately and with calm conviction, "I want each of you to know that I love you, and that you can call me anytime, day or night, if you need anything."

I don't think I ever called him, but I remember the invitation. It was like someone giving you blank checks from a fat bank account. This man seemed to know that the one thing everybody needs is intentional care. Whether he realized it or not, the invitation itself was a deposit of love, especially for an adolescent like me who didn't have a father.

WHAT WE CRAVE TO FIND IN OTHERS

Stop and think about the people who have made the deepest impressions on you, in the sense that the stamp of their character left certain marks on yours. Those marks may be positive characteristics like honesty, courage, or wisdom, or they may be negative characteristics like irresponsibility, self-centeredness, or volatility.

There is one character trait, however, that we all crave to find in others. It is a trait some people possess that inspires us to trust them, depend on them, get life energy from them, run to them when we're wounded, and think about them when we're alone. That trait is love, and it doesn't show up as an occasional spectacular event but as the consistent, repetitive design—the pattern—of a person's life.

Don't think of love as frilly sentiment or adolescent infatuation. Love is the gutsiest and boldest of human initiatives. It is a casting of oneself forward, a costly expenditure of life for the benefit of others. Think of one of those terrified young men running up the blood-stained beach on D day, propelled forward toward the ultimate sacrifice, and then remember Jesus' words about the greatest love: "Greater love has no one than this, that he lay down his life for his friends" (John 15:13).

Of course, not every day is D day. Still, love as an everyday pattern is a true "laying down" of one's life in dozens of smaller acts of personal giving.

What would happen if multitudes of people of faith prayed every day: "Lord, make me—before all else, and above all else—a person who loves"? What if we set aside all our images of what a mature spiritual life looks like and boiled it all down to this: Am I growing in love? Despite all the complexities of spiritual life, Jesus was able to give us a singular vision, one great commandment.

Let's consider two questions. What exactly is the shape of love? And what can I do to make it the pulse of my own life?

THE MOST EXCELLENT WAY

The Bible calls love "the most excellent way" (1 Cor. 12:31). Of the few things in our lives that can echo for eternity (faith, hope, and love), the greatest is love. And this is its shape (from "the love chapter," 1 Corinthians 13):

1. Love is mature considerateness ("love is patient, love is kind"). Love is being as aware of the other person as we are of ourselves, giving some slack where we can and cheering the other person on.
2. Love is confident selflessness ("it does not envy, it does not boast, it is not proud"). Love looks out at others, out at the world, and finds in that vision things that are far more interesting than the self. Love is the pleasure of bragging about other people instead of making a big noise about yourself.
3. Love is charitable awareness ("it is not rude, it is not self-seeking"). It gives us a distaste for advancing ourselves at the expense of others. Love has good manners.
4. Love is forbearance and forgiveness ("it is not easily angered, it keeps no record of wrongs"). Love means being a coach, not a referee.
5. Love is wholesome expectation ("love does not delight in evil but rejoices with the truth"). We show love when we cheer others on in their victories and when we feel wounded when we witness their failures.
6. Love is protective concern ("it always protects, always trusts"). Love makes gossip bitter in our mouths and prompts us instead to add to the good reputation of others.
7. Love is optimistic commitment ("it always hopes, always perseveres, love never fails"). Love means hoping for the best, not as naive optimism or wishful thinking but as an expectation that God can and does do great things because "he fills everything in every way."

No wonder love is the most excellent way.

To Flow Through, It Has to Flow To

Put it all together and this is the shape of unfailing love. What makes love so strong, so enduring, and so trustworthy? What makes it the backbone of creatures who are meant to walk upright?

It's not that people who love give and those who are loveless are concerned only with receiving. People who love have a developed ability to vigorously give *and* receive.

You've certainly seen plenty of examples of the receive-only person, and there is an abundance of adjectives for such people: self-centered, self-absorbed, self-important, self-satisfied, selfish. And you've probably run into the give-only kind of love. This is the limited love of those whose self-imposed martyrdom means they will serve others until exhausted but expect in return obligation and sympathy, not joy. This is a pale, sickly kind of love, and it does more to empty everybody involved than to fill them. If somebody expects us to feel sorry for him because of what he did for us, perhaps the gift should not have been given in the first place.

Biblical love is a steady and powerful flow of God's grace into and through human personality. It is receiving and giving. This is the big picture of 1 Corinthians 13. People who really love never feel taken advantage of because they know—when no one else but God knows—just how deeply they have drunk from the well of God's love.

Love is a settled disposition that says, "The reason I have a life is because of an act of God's love, and the only reason I can survive the pains and wounds in this life, including my own stupid mistakes and shortcomings, is because God is love. He gives me every breath and every meal that passes over my tongue. He forgives my sin. He inspires me to hope for high things. He is the mover behind every good action in this world. Therefore, I am compelled to love him, and I must love others because he loves them so much. Love is a mission God has given me. And there is no greater satisfaction than to feel spent because God allowed me to give away some of my time and energy for someone else today."

EVERYDAY LOVE

So how can love become an everyday reality in our lives? It won't happen through theoretical talk or pious principles. We need to ask God to pour his love over the edges of our lives into the lives of others, realizing that we will always have a self-protective resistance in us that says, "Don't bother, don't expend, don't slow down." And then we need to step forward when opportunities come. This is the face of love in the everyday:

- Listen twice as much as you talk.
- When you think you've listened, check just to make sure.
- Pray for a person who really irritates you.
- Let someone know when he or she has done a really good thing.
- Consider a quality hour invested in the life of a child as being worth a hundred hours in years to come.
- Choose not to respond to rudeness with rudeness.
- Throw away written reminders of wrongs done to you.
- If you're married, care for your spouse as Christ cares for the church.
- Look for opportunities to "feed" others any good insights or wisdom God has given you. (Note Jesus' words: "Feed my lambs," John 21:15).
- Take time to offer guidance to people who are wandering in their lives (but only offer guidance based on the wisdom of God, so that it is not the blind leading the blind).
- Tell your faith story to someone who has no real concept of how God can be a part of our lives.
- When you're driving, let other people merge into your lane when they need to.
- Confidently say no to someone who is out of control because all he has ever heard is "Yes" or "I don't care."
- Visit someone in the hospital who doesn't expect you.
- Send cards or email with a sentence or two of encouragement.
- If you're a parent, consider your kids' growing-up years a season of unique self-sacrifice.

- Treat your aging parents as elders, even if they're dependent on you.
- Don't make yourself the center of conversation. Ask people questions about themselves.
- Tell someone you will pray for him or her only when you really intend to do so.
- When you're talking to someone, look him or her square in the eye.
- If you don't know what to say to someone who is suffering intensely, let him know that he is frequently on your mind. Use a hug or a firm handshake with two hands to say what words cannot say.

LIVING WITHOUT LOVE

How important is the pattern of love? Just ask yourself how anxious you are to be around people who have no love to offer. Do you enthusiastically respond to their invitation to dinner? Do you stay around people who berate you? How likely are you to linger in a part of town where gang warfare can erupt any minute?

Living without love is to be something less than a human being. As the apostle Paul put it at the beginning of the love chapter, If I don't have love, I'm just one big noise ("a resounding gong or a clanging symbol"), and even if I give up my life in a great heroic act, if I don't have love, my sacrifice counts as nothing ("I am nothing"). To live a God-filled life is to live a love-filled life. And maybe someday somebody will choose to engrave a couple of simple words on your tombstone—Loving Father, Mother, Son, Sister, or Friend.

PRACTICE THIS

Each day when you are walking among other people, say a brief silent prayer for each person you pass, whether you know them or not. See if you can look at other people as Jesus might see them. Take a few moments to reflect on what your attitude really is toward other people.

FOR PERSONAL REFLECTION

1. Read 1 Corinthians 13 in three different translations.

2. Give as many concrete examples as you can of the seven groupings of characteristics from 1 Corinthians 13:
   - "Love is patient, love is kind."
   - "It does not envy, it does not boast, it is not proud."
   - "It is not rude, it is not self-seeking."
   - "It is not easily angered, it keeps no record of wrongs."
   - "Love does not delight in evil but rejoices with the truth."
   - "It always protects, it always trusts."
   - "It always hopes, always perseveres. Love never fails."

3. What is the difference between loving people and just being nice to them? In other words, what is the difference between active love and a benign, passive kind of love?

4. Since love is always a challenge, what is the biggest challenge and the biggest opportunity you are facing right now in loving someone? How can others pray for you in this?

BEYOND ENJOYMENT

Joy

Last year my thirteen-year-old son and I invaded Disneyland in southern California for an exhausting day and a half. He set the pace, so we sometimes ran from one attraction to the next. Drenched on some water rides, nauseated by the dropping rides, and just plain thrilled by the adventure rides, we barely took time to eat and certainly not to rest. We bragged (with some blatant macho) that things would have been much different if Mom or Eva had been along. I had long needed to spend some private time with my son, and I knew that this kind of enjoyment would be a great break for both of us. But the real joy for me in this experience was not in the enjoyment.

The real joy for me came as I looked over at my son on the way home, strapped in by his seatbelt, earphones stuck in his ears, a dazed look on his face, and his eyelids sinking slowly despite his struggle to stay awake for every last moment. It was the joy not of doing something enjoyable but of knowing a bit of the goodness of God in giving us each other.

A PATTERN OF PEACEABLE CONCLUSIONS

Enjoyment comes in many forms. We may enjoy a trip to a new place, a day of warm sun or of cooling breezes, a pleasant evening with friends. Enjoyment happens when a really great meal stimulates our taste buds, when our ears take in a pleasing song, or when we smell the raw scent of the ocean. But joy is a settled state of the soul. It is something that comes because of an understanding of life developed over a long period of time, a pattern of peaceable conclusions.

The Bible talks about being filled with joy, and that has so much to do with living a God-filled life. When God helps us realize just how much he has filled our lives, that's when the real filling of joy comes.

Joy is a sense of glad certitude that comes when we witness something that is very right—the way things are *meant* to be—or when we have the privilege of making something right happen. Joy is when we say, "Aha! Yes, I see it now," as if a sufficient number of jigsaw puzzle pieces have come together to reveal the whole picture of what life should be. Joy is when you have a conviction that says, "Yes, *this* is what it means to be a parent," or "I know this must have been done directly by God," or "I am so weary, but I'm glad to have been able to serve today in a way that is really right for who God made me to be." And then you pause and try to figure out why you have the joy that you do. What have you discovered?

Joy means having settled the accounts of your life with God, realizing what you can do and what you cannot do and coming to believe that the key to life is to open your eyes and watch what God is doing all around you. How else could a man in prison nearing execution say, "Rejoice in the Lord always. I will say it again: Rejoice!" (Philippians 4:4). Amazing! Because real joy goes deep, it is beyond the merely sensible: "Though you have not seen him, you love him; and even though you do not see him now, you believe in him and are filled with an inexpressible and glorious joy" (1 Peter 1:8).

A SATISFYING HUNGER

More than happiness, much more than pleasure, joy is a taste of the knowledge of God, and thus it is a kind of longing, a spiritual hunger that is satisfying even in its hunger. That is why Psalm 34:8 says, "Taste and see that the LORD is good." God doesn't invite us to admire him from afar or to hold him as a set of principles, like a constitution preserved on yellowed parchment. He says, "Taste." In other words, we are to take in and experience who God is and what he does. That's also why Jesus said, "Take and eat," "Take and drink." He wants his own goodness to go deeply into us. The biblical word for grace *(charis)* is closely related to the word for joy *(chara)*. God's grace in our lives emerges as joy.

PRACTICING JOY

So how can joy be an often-repeated experience, such that it becomes part of our character? Here are some things to think about.

- *Let joy happen; don't seek it for its own sake.* Joy does not come out of thin air. It is a state of one's heart that develops from many cumulative experiences of the goodness and grace of God. You might meet someone new, for instance, who adds a delightful insight to your day. Look for a new activity to share with your family that nobody ever thought of doing before. Offer to serve in a ministry of your church or serve in your community in a way that you have never thought of serving before.
- *Receive all gifts of God with gratitude.* Saying thank you to God many times a week is a way of opening our eyes to just how many blessings he has poured out on us. We know about thanking God for our food, but what about thanking God for a good conversation with a friend, a time of worship, a graduation ceremony, a good night's sleep, a day of work, or a time of quiet prayer? Gratitude gives birth to joy.
- *Celebrate!* The Old Testament has at least a dozen different root words for joy (exult, rejoice, sing aloud, shout, and so

on). Joy should be regularly released, especially in enthusiastic public worship. Take every opportunity in public celebrations (graduations, weddings, award events) to help the person being honored to sense the grace of God in it all. You may be the only person who will give a meaningful gift or write a card that is truly insightful.

- *Enjoy every pleasure that is a gift of God.* Realize what the pleasures of the senses point us to. God gave us five senses so that we could survive in this world but also so that we would be vitally conscious of all the dimensions of his creation and in turn praise the Creator.

- *Take pleasure in the higher things that please God.* Enjoyment of the creation is one thing, but this enjoyment should lead us to long for the great moral qualities of God, which he wants to impress on us. God is pleased when we act something like the dignified creatures we were created to be, when we focus on "whatever is true, whatever is noble, whatever is right, whatever is pure, whatever is lovely, whatever is admirable . . . excellent or praiseworthy" (Phil. 4:8). So joy comes when you help someone confused come to a realization of the truth of the situation, when you treat as noble someone who is being beaten up by someone else. Joy comes when you see a movie that has an admirable theme or when you read the story of someone who did something of moral praiseworthiness.

- *Take an accounting of reality when pain and trials come.* Probably every person who has read James 1:2 is confused at first: "Consider it pure joy . . . whenever you face trials of many kinds." Another translation puts it this way: "Whenever trouble comes your way, let it be an opportunity for joy" (NLT). How can God expect us to rejoice when we just want to scream?

The Bible never gives a command to be happy. On Mount Sinai God did not say, "Thou shalt always have a smile on thy face." Happiness, like all emotions, comes and goes. What James is saying is this: whenever you are on the knife's edge of tough decisions, whenever you go through the trials of loss or disappointment, stop and take a serious spiritual accounting of all reality. God is still real. His glory and goodness are not diminished. Going through a trial might seem like going into the dusk and then the blackness of night. But the sun never stops shining. God never ceases to be God. And because of that, the night will always be pushed back by the light of day in due course.

- *Do not sabotage the goodness of God.* From a practical standpoint, we must not sabotage our enjoyment of the goodness of God with any kind of substance abuse, which messes up all perceptions. We must not crowd out the enjoyment of God by so many material concerns that there just is no space for the spiritual. We should take time to read Scripture and other uplifting literature that has spiritual substance. We should find time to get out into the natural world, where we can see the exuberance of God.

- *Make Christ the center of your joy.* In the New Testament Jesus was the fountainhead of joy. His presence inspired joy in Mary, the angels, the shepherds, the Magi. He entered Jerusalem for the last time enveloped in the rejoicing of the people, and on the third day after his death, "the women hurried away from the tomb, afraid yet filled with joy" (Matt. 28:8). That certainly wasn't the last time someone was amazed to find joy and fear occupying the same space and somehow defining each other.

PRACTICE THIS

Between waking in the morning and going to bed at night, find at least five times during the day when you say to God, "I rejoice because . . ."

FOR PERSONAL REFLECTION

1. If someone came to you and said, "I want some of the joy that I see in you—how can I get that?" what would you say? How would you describe joy to this person?

2. What are some things that give a passing experience of enjoyment but leave us with less joy?

3. Describe something in your life that time and again has produced a sense of joy in your life. (For instance, vacations, worship, quality time with friends.) Why did that give you joy?

4. When in your life have joyful moments seemed few and far between? What did you do to get through that time?

5. What does it mean to rejoice even when you don't have an awareness of joy?

THE TRANQUILITY OF ORDER

Peace

Some people walked the streets of Rome dazed and dumbfounded. Others scurried close to the walls like rats trying to keep out of sight. From atop the walls wearied soldiers shot arrows randomly and to little effect. When the raiding army finally broke through the gate, the soldiers began setting fire to houses.

It was on a summer day, August 24, in the year 410 that the unthinkable happened to the citizens of the great city of Rome. For three long days the Visigothic king, Alaric, had besieged the city until finally the gates flew open, and for the first time in eight hundred years a foreign army occupied and plundered the city. This was the beginning of the end of the Western Roman Empire, and many Romans blamed the now numerous Christians for upsetting the gods and bringing on the disaster.

PEACE AS ORDER

The great Christian leader and theologian, Augustine of Hippo, replied to this charge, saying that Christians were not to blame for calamity, neither were the pagan gods responsible for good fortune. The world consists of those who belong to the City of Man (because their first love is themselves) and those who belong to the City of God (because their first love is God).

Where can we find peace in a world so beset with tensions and conflicts? Augustine offered a compelling definition. He called peace the "tranquility of order."

If peace is the tranquility of order, it is so much more than just the absence of conflict. If a husband and wife stop their quarrels and shouting matches only to fall into icy indifference, do they have peace? If a boss and his former employee settle a lawsuit out of court, is that peace? And what about spiritual conflict? If a person who has been wrestling with painful doubts and unanswered spiritual questions finally becomes numb to it all, does that mean that he has come to a place of peace?

God has something much better in mind for us than just the lessening of conflict in our lives. Health doesn't just mean not having broken bones or not having a black eye. We long for much more than that. Deep inside we are looking for an orderliness of our thoughts and passions, our motives and aspirations. And when we can experience that, even if it is incomplete or passing, we will have a sense of peace—the tranquility of order.

How can you have order in your life when there is disorder all around you? Order is a life pattern. When we say to God, "Please, oh please, help me get my life in order," that is an appeal for divine assistance to get things sorted out, to understand what is important, what thoughts and motives need to be thrown out, what matters to put at the top of the priority list, what good habits to develop and stick with. Peace has to be a pattern, because occasional and tentative cease-fires produce neither contentment nor virtue.

FIRST STEPS TOWARD PEACE

Peace begins with our relationship with God. If you're fighting with God or if there is a cold war going on between you and God, then the un-tranquility of disorder is going to be the pattern of your life. Why should that be? Why can't a human being say to God, "I'll just leave you alone, you leave me alone, and everything will be fine"? That doesn't work (never has, never will, never could) because the very order of the universe is based on the relationship of the Creator and the created. God, who is spectacularly glorious and good, benevolent and powerful, who is the master craftsman, brought the whole universe into being and put human beings right at the top of the whole order. And he still stands over it all, proud of what is good, and especially of what is "very good." He is pained by the cracks and flaws that have been introduced into the creation, but he is ready to heal and one day recreate it. This is the order of all things. This order is where we can find tranquility. Live like you're an animal, and you won't have peace; live like you're God, and you won't have peace. Peace is the continual rehearsal of standing in the right spot in the grand order of things—not lower, not higher. Alaric didn't know that. And what determines if we are barbarians is not whether we know how to dress, eat, and write letters but whether we accept our proper place in the universe.

THE GIFT OF SHALOM

The Hebrews greeted each other with a single word of well-wishing, a kind of prayer that prays it all: *Shalom*, which means "peace to you." It is not merely saying, "I hope nobody beats you up today," but rather, "May you enjoy security and safety, may you experience harmony and accord in all parts of your life, and may you have soundness, completeness, and health in every respect." What could be better in your life than to have shalom, not just once in a great while but as the tempo of your life?

How do we develop a pattern of peace?

Let's begin with Jesus' words: "Peace I leave with you; my peace I give you. I do not give to you as the world gives. Do not let your hearts be troubled and do not be afraid" (John 14:27). There is a peace that the world gives, but the peace of Jesus is different.

A good friend of mine, Bob, was in the Pacific theater during World War II. His young wife, Win, waited anxiously to get each letter so that she could be assured he was still alive. Bob made it through the battle of Guadalcanal and all the rest and returned home when "peace" had been achieved in 1945. How bewildered Bob and Win were, like so many other families, when they were torn apart again a mere five years later so that the young men could board ships bound, this time, for Korea. Five years. Then came the end of the Korean War. The guns stopped, but was it peace?

Last year I had the privilege of meeting with and teaching among the dynamic Christians of South Korea. One day they drove me to the infamous 38th parallel, the two-mile-wide demilitarized zone between North and South Korea, one of the tensest places in the world. Wall after wall of curled, razor-wire fences, concrete barriers, and one lookout tower after another with soldiers peering across the valley. A sign stating that this was a military zone warned against making any sudden or suspicious movements and banned any camera out of its case. The mood of the whole place seemed heavy with fear and antagonism.

The peace the world gives is often just a time for reloading.

Jesus was about to leave his disciples, knowing that they would witness the horror of his slow execution, but he wanted to let them know that his final act on earth would bring a permanent peace. He left them violently, but he left them with the promise of peace. And days after his blood had dried at the base of his cross, a resurrected Jesus appeared to his disciples and picked up where he had left off, as he greeted them with the most ordinary and most extraordinary words: "Peace be with you."

LORD OF PEACE

Paul said, "We have peace with God through our Lord Jesus Christ" (Rom. 5:1). He explained that this peace came "through his blood, shed on the cross" (Col. 1:20). Paul poured out his well-wishing whenever he wrote, longing for people to experience real peace: "Now may the Lord of peace himself give you peace at all times and in every way" (2 Thess. 3:16); "May the God of hope fill you with all joy and peace as you trust in him" (Rom. 15:13). Why? Because "God is not a God of disorder but of peace" (1 Cor. 14:33). And so our mandate is to set patterns of peace in our lives: "If it is possible, as far as it depends on you, live at peace with everyone" (Rom. 12:18); "Let us therefore make every effort to do what leads to peace and to mutual edification" (Rom. 14:19). When we promote peace, we experience peace: "And the peace of God, which transcends all understanding, will guard your hearts and your minds in Christ Jesus" (Phil. 4:7). "Blessed are the peacemakers," Jesus said, because they really are children of God.

EXPERIENCING TRANQUILITY

Here are some things we can do to experience the tranquility of order.

1. *Value peace in your relationships.* If it matters little to us whether our lives are full of conflict or full of peace, then we will not work toward peace. Some people who have grown up with a lot of conflict in their lives are actually unsettled if there isn't tension in the air. Realize that if you value order in your relationships, you are giving a great gift to other people. You are saying to them, "You are valuable enough to me that I will do the work necessary to keep our accounts settled."

2. *Do as much as you can to promote peace in your relationships, but realize that you are limited in what you can do.* The Bible gives us a very realistic assessment when it says, "As far as it depends on you, live at peace with everyone" (Rom. 12:18). In other words, you can only do what you can do. Sometimes no matter how hard you try to resolve a dispute or settle a tension with someone else, it just doesn't happen, because the other person doesn't do what he or she needs to do. You cannot accomplish peace at any price. If you sacrifice truth for the sake of peace, you will have a fragile resolution at best and you will be even less likely to find real peace the next time around.

3. *If you feel your life is full of disorder, pick one or two very specific areas that can provide some structure in your life.* Focus on one relationship that is working well or on one role you are

doing well. It may even help to focus on putting one room in your house in order. Years ago when I was trying to begin my doctoral dissertation, I was stuck, just plain stuck. One problem was that I felt many areas of my life were in a state of disorder. I wasn't on top of things in my work at the church, the house wasn't in order, my wife and I weren't spending enough time together. Then one Saturday I decided to bring order to the most disorderly part of our household: our garage. I really dug in. I threw out every junkie thing I shouldn't hold on to, found a place for every tool, and neatly arranged the glue, the rope, the ladder, and everything else. When that chaos turned to order—in just that one small part of my life—I was able to turn to other areas of my life and do the same, one area at a time. And best of all, I finally took control of that nasty dissertation project. I believe to this day that cleaning out my garage was an integral step in getting my dissertation done. In this life there will always be a fair amount of disorder, of course, but a basic sense of the grand order of things will enable us to taste the peace that goes beyond understanding.

4. *Do not confuse peace with an obsessive, controlling desire for order.* If you know you have a somewhat compulsive personality and you know that you frustrate others by insisting that they order themselves according to your standards, then stop and assess what *kind* of order you are looking for in life. We don't achieve peace when we drive other people crazy by fastidiously trying to iron every wrinkle out of life. "A place for everything and everything in its place" may be a good general principle, but we need to realize that life is always in flux. Things move. People come and go. Sometimes you get the items on your list checked off and sometimes not. The most important things to keep in order ("as far as it depends on you"!) are your relationships—first with God, then with your family, then with others. You can hope and expect that others will try to conform to God's standards for order, but their own standards for order may be different from yours, which may not apply to them.

5. *Open your eyes to the order of the Creation.* Reflecting on the Creation will remind you that God creates order and thus he also creates harmony and interdependence. Yes, there are disorderly things in nature, such as earthquakes, forest fires, and floods. But the ordinary face of creation is a perpetual essay about the natural tranquility that God values and about the goal he has charged human beings to pursue. To study the Creation is to read a book God has put right in front of our eyes. Written in the book of nature are truths about uniformity and variety, growth and development. The Creation leads to the ultimate personality and mind that conceived and willed it into existence. The tranquility of order comes from growing in your understanding of your own creatureliness. Humanity does not stand apart from creation but is part of it, so we should learn about how God orders life by studying how he orders the Creation.

6. *Take advantage of the periods of peace you enjoy in life.* There will be many times in our lives when we wrestle with conflicts, grieve losses, or endure pain. When we are in calm waters, however, we should make the most of it and learn about the way things ought to be. When our relationships are in good order, we should reflect on that and develop our convictions about what peace is and how we can preserve the tranquility of order.

PRAY THIS

Dear Lord, I need your help today because I don't always see the perfection of your order in this world and in my life. Help me to have faith at all times that you are in control, and help me to trust your promise of peace in my life. Help me to be a peacelover and a peacemaker. Forgive me for all the times when I have engaged in fights with others. Show me in new ways that you have already won the war against evil. As the final battles move toward the end, help me to be an ambassador of your peace, glad to be in your service. Amen.

FOR PERSONAL REFLECTION

1. Which areas of your life now seem, or have seemed in the past, like major battles instead of peace?

2. When have you experienced the peace of God in your life? Did this peace appear instantaneously after a long struggle? Did peace come because you did something?

3. When is it difficult for you to trust in the peace of Christ? Can you identify why it is difficult to trust Christ's peace at that particular time?

4. With God's help, what specific steps could you take in the weeks to come to set patterns of order and peace in your life?

5. How can others pray for you?

WILLING TO WAIT

Patience

I don't like hearing that I need to be patient. And I know why: because I do not *like* to be patient. Yet I know I must try to be patient because I'm counting on everybody else in my life to be patient with me.

If there is a problem to be solved, my natural inclination is to want it to be solved *now*. If there is something I want to achieve or obtain, I'd like to have it *now*. I tried building model airplanes as a kid, but I was never good at it because I wanted to skip the stage-by-stage instructions, glue the whole thing together right away, slap those decals on, and stick it on the stand. I once launched a fat two-foot-high model rocket before the glue had completely dried. When it came apart ten feet off the ground it became a wildly erratic unguided missile, which caused my sister and two cousins to run for cover. I, of course, blamed it on mechanical failure, not wanting to admit to my sister and cousins that I flew the doggone thing thirty minutes after I built it.

Now that I am an adult, my impatience is about far more serious things. Why can't people change faster? Why don't I change faster? Will I make it to the end of the book I'm reading? Will

I make it to the end of this book I'm writing? How are my kids going to turn out—in their hearts and souls? Why don't my skills in ministry grow faster?

THE PROBLEM WITH "NOW"

"Now" is a golden calf of the modern world. The proverb "All good things are worth waiting for" seems like a dusty old sentiment that must have come from someone who lacked either ambition or creativity. What is progress in the world if not the advancing ability to make "now" even more "now"? *Later* is an ugly sounding word. Delayed gratification seems like nonsense.

I remember my wife and I trying to teach our young children about the strange concept of "later."

"Can I have some of my candy?"

"No, not now. Later."

Which always prompted the rejoinder: "*When* later?"

"I don't know, just later."

"But *when* later?"

We should have known better. We need to know that we have to be patient not merely for the arbitrary reason of waiting until later. When there are specific and good reasons to wait for the candy or the new car or to pursue your education, develop a courtship, or establish your career, we should talk about the reasons. Patience is necessary because *time* is the track along which life runs, and you get to your destination by going one mile at a time.

THE COURAGE TO ENDURE

There are two different kinds of patience. One is the *courage to endure*. The opposite of cowardice or despondency, this kind of patience is what gets people through real hardship, whether pain or provocation. It is an attitude that says, "With God's help, I *am* going to get through this one way or another."

Patient comes from a Latin word meaning "to bear pain," which is why we call a person in a hospital bed a patient. But as anyone who has worked in a health care facility can tell you, there are patient patients, and not-so-patient patients. It takes courage to endure suffering, and we should never take for granted the courage of those who are suffering. They need to receive a steady flow of sincere compassion; they need patience from us while they try to be patient. Those who show the courage to endure deserve our honor. They are some of our most important teachers.

THE WILLINGNESS TO WAIT

The other kind of patience is the *willingness to wait.* A more everyday kind of patience, this pattern of attitude and action comes from the belief that most of the good things in life develop gradually and progressively. The best things in life *are* worth waiting for. In a single day or week a child grows just a little, someone's faith develops a bit more, a developing character becomes just a little more solid. Waiting is a high-level skill. It is not merely "waiting around," as you might wait for the next bus to come to the bus stop. The willingness to wait is a form of expectation. It is an attitude that says, "I have to live life; I can't force it to happen. It won't kill me to wait. I may even learn a thing or two while I'm waiting."

Some people believe in *carpe diem:* "Seize the day! Don't let opportunity pass you by. Don't be left in the dust." I agree, with some qualification. Being decisive and jumping on an opportunity is a good thing. We just need to make sure that we are seizing today, not tomorrow. We should make sure today doesn't pass us by, while making equally sure we don't try to live tomorrow today. Isn't this what Jesus meant when he said, "Therefore do not worry about tomorrow, for tomorrow will worry about itself. Each day has enough trouble of its own" (Matt. 6:34)?

Those who grow crops understand waiting. Seed to seedling, seedling to shoot, shoot to plant, plant to harvest. Plow and cultivate and wait. Wait for the sun, the rain, and the energies of nature in the seeds to do the work, and you will be rewarded. You invest some money and a lot of sweat, but mostly you wait with patience for the natural course of things to unfold. James 5:7 says, "Be patient, then, brothers, until the Lord's coming. See how the farmer waits for the land to yield its valuable crop and how patient he is for the autumn and spring rains."

WHAT ALTERNATIVE DO WE HAVE?

Spouses have to be patient with each other. How else could marriage possibly work? Parents need to exercise purposeful waiting as they help their children step from one new challenge to the next. All of us need to be patient as we forbear the rough edges of each other's personalities. If human beings came with warning labels, they'd all have to say, "Handle with care; may cause injury."

And when conflicts do occur and we do the best we can to clean up the mess, we need to wait for the healing effects of time. Why do we say "Time heals"? It's not because the calendar has power, or even that we hope that forgetfulness will move across our minds like a fog. Time has a healing effect because the God-designed healing powers within body and soul do their inexorable work—but gradually.

What good alternative do we have to patience? Getting red-faced and stomping our feet accomplishes nothing. Settling into being angry with the world and with most of the people who inhabit it just makes us bitter. Throwing our hands up in pessimism and despondency will blind us to real progress. Patience may not come easily, but there is no good alternative.

Courage to endure and willingness to wait are not acts of resignation. Patience is a conscious and deliberate strategy for life. It is fundamentally a spiritual movement.

FAITH, HOPE, AND LOVE IN ACTION

Patience is faith, hope, and love in action. The Bible says that these are the realities that remain when everything else passes away (1 Cor. 13:13).

Patience is faith in action because it says:

• I believe God is in control of life.

• I believe God has given you great potential.
• I believe trust is basic to life.

Patience is hope in action because it says:

• I expect that God has great things in mind for the future.
• Today's hurt will not remain forever.
• I know that right will prevail over wrong.

Patience is love in action because it says:

• You are worth waiting for.
• Thanks for putting up with my many faults.
• I know you don't always mean what you say.
• I'll get over being disappointed.

When we don't feel like being patient, one of the best things we can do is to consider the great patience of God. "The Lord is not slow in keeping his promise, as some understand slowness. He is patient with you, not wanting anyone to perish, but everyone to come to repentance" (2 Peter 3:9). On either side of this truth lie two great errors in the way people think about God. The first error is thinking that God is impatient, capricious, and ready to pounce on our failures. The second is thinking that God is removed and indifferent. The truth is that God is engaged in this world, he wants the best for us, and he is willing to wait and give us every possible chance to respond appropriately to him. God is also patient in that he is "slow to anger." Moses heard these words about God: "The LORD, the LORD, the compassionate and gracious God, slow to anger, abounding in love and faithfulness, maintaining love to thousands, and forgiving wickedness, rebellion and sin. Yet he does not leave the guilty unpunished" (Ex. 34:6–7). Patience is the difference between someone who wants to be angry and feeds it and someone who becomes appropriately angry because of real evil or wrongdoing.

Patience is a mark of real character. It is the fruit of believing the right things about God, ourselves, and our future. It is an antidote to attitudes of revenge, competitiveness, scrutiny, and harsh judgment. Patience loosens the choking grip of anxiety and worry. It is the generous gift of tolerance. Patience makes the effort to understand and does not watch the clock or the calendar. Patience is the restraint of impulse.

BETTER THAN COUNTING TO TEN

So how can we practice a pattern of patience? Here are some practical things we can do.

1. When confronting a frustrating situation, distinguish what you can do from what you have no power over.
2. In prayer, ask God to help you release your grip on troubling situations.
3. When you want someone to be different, realize that although you may try to exercise appropriate influence, it is not your responsibility to change someone else.
4. When you've said your peace, rest in that.
5. Forbear simple annoyances.
6. When you are enduring suffering, find the anchors that will hold you steady for the long haul, keep trusting, and tell others and God when you sense trust is slipping away.

Does there come a time when patience is rightfully at an end?

At the conclusion of our worship services in our church we always invite people who have a prayer need to step up and pray with one of the pastors about their needs. More often than not, the kinds of things I pray with people about are those frustrating, tension-producing struggles in life that are just going to require faith and patience. I often talk to people who have been patient for a very long time—with an ill-tempered spouse, a wayward teenager, or an interfering in-law. They usually wonder, "Is there something I've neglected to do, some prayer I haven't prayed?"

Sometimes we have waited a long time for someone to make right choices, but then the time for waiting is over. We make our decisions and move on. But that doesn't mean patience has come to an end; it just means that patience has run its course. Patience means letting a process work its way to an appropriate end.

But we need to be ready. There is always one more episode of frustration just around the corner, when we will once again have to find God's power to help us endure and wait.

PRAY THIS

> God, help me to wait.
> God, help me to endure.
> God, thank you for being so patient with me.
> Amen.

FOR PERSONAL REFLECTION

1. In what kinds of situations do you find it hardest to be patient? (For example, parenting, marriage, work, friendships, caring for parents.)

2. Describe someone who has blessed you by being patient with you.

3. What is the difference between being patient and just being easygoing?

4. In what ways has God been patient with you?

5. Who can you pray for right now who is suffering and needs the courage to endure?

6. How can others pray for you to have patience?

MUCH MORE THAN A SMILE

Kindness

8

C an you wiggle your toes? Press your foot as hard as you can against my hand."

Those were some of the most unsettling words I've ever heard, because I knew they meant that someone was checking to see if I had a spinal cord injury. I didn't know who it was, because I was just regaining consciousness. I was aware that I was on my back on some kind of a stretcher, the sun was in my eyes, my head felt like it was in a vise, and my body hurt everywhere. A couple of people in white shirts were staring down at me, and I could hear the voices of others around me, including my wife's voice. "Yes, I can follow in my own car," she said to someone. Then one of the men staring down told me I had been in a bike accident, I had a head injury, and they would be taking me to the hospital. My glasses were gone— smashed into the pavement—my face was bleeding from an open gash above my eye, my lip was severed, my collar bone was broken, and my ribs were severely bruised. I remember thinking, "Wait a minute—I don't do hospitals. I'm a pastor; I *visit* people in hospitals." Lesson number one on bike riding: When you fly headfirst over the handlebars of your bike and break your fall with your forehead, the pavement wins every time.

At that moment and during the next three days in the hospital and the following weeks of recovery from a severe concussion, I learned more about kindness than I had in years. I had to have dependency forced on me to learn about kindness. It began with the man in the truck who came upon me in the middle of the road just a minute after my accident and called the emergency number on his cellular phone. Amazingly, this man was a member of our church, so the second phone call he made put a rapid-fire prayer chain in motion. Dozens of people were already praying for me before the paramedics loaded me into the ambulance!

The paramedics were angels of mercy who put up with my confused babbling all the way to the hospital. Kindness was the gift of the people in the neighborhood where my accident happened who helped take care of my son, who was the only one with me when it happened. A surgeon friend arrived at the hospital shortly after the ambulance did and ordered the X rays, consulted with a couple of other doctors, did some fine stitching, and admitted me to the hospital.

Abundant kindness. Although "kindness" might not be the word I'd use for the X-ray technicians whose room seemed like a meat locker and who pushed and pulled my body in ways that I considered greatly inconvenient at the time. But I suppose that is their special form of kindness.

It happened to be bicycle safety week, and lots of friends, with a form of gleeful kindness, brought special bicycle safety posters up to my room. I also received cards, many cards. I got back in full all the dollars I had spent on get-well cards over the years. Every one of them was a small installment of kindness, and it added up to a treasure.

My wife and my kids served me for days, let me sleep most of the time—which is all you want to do when your brain is trying to heal itself—and for several months put up with my unpredictable limitations, mood swings, and general lack of self-awareness.

It is said that a little bit of kindness goes a long way. How true that is. I needed a little bit—many times over.

KINDNESS IS . . .

The Bible teaches that kindness is generosity, good will, mercy, and especially love toward people in distress. Kindness streams out of a person's life when that person has allowed God's kindness to stream into his life. God delights in exercising kindness (Jer. 9:24). He leads his people "with cords of human kindness, with ties of love" (Hos. 11:4). We should not take for granted "the riches of [God's] kindness, tolerance and patience," because it is God's kindness that leads us toward him (Rom. 2:4).

We do not live in a kind world. Basic human selfishness often puts quills on our backs that we think protect us but that only hurt others. Damaged human beings often just go around damaging others. Greed, power, and untamed passion make for a grabby, not a generous, world. Consider how many words we have for unkindness: crabby, irritable, nasty, surly, cranky, cross, disagreeable, petulant, bad-tempered, inconsiderate, unsympathetic, cantankerous, grouchy, grumpy, ill-tempered, irascible, testy. What a vocabulary we need for our native roughness.

KINDNESS APPEARED

Yet one day Kindness himself appeared. To be more specific, "the kindness and love of God our Savior appeared" (Titus 3:4). Jesus Christ, who shows "the incomparable riches of [God's] grace (Eph. 2:7), is the Divine Kindness who showed up just in time to save us— each of us—who can be so unkind.

When we are in deep trouble we long to see some rescuer suddenly appear—the firefighter at an inferno, the paramedics at the scene of an accident, the police at a hostage crisis, the coast guard when your boat is ready to sink. Suddenly, decisively, kindness appears. And it is not the kindness of soft words or a gentle smile but a strong act of intervention, a mighty deliverance and salvation. So it was when Christ came to save us: "When the kindness and love of God our Savior appeared, he saved us, not because of righteous things we had done, but because of his mercy."

RETURNING KINDNESS

It is a gift beyond measure to receive mercy, especially when you're in trouble, but it is so easy to forget to return the favor.

Consider this: on any given day in any given situation, you may be the one person in the right spot to make kindness appear before someone's eyes. Your kindness may startle that person or he may hardly notice it. Either way, obedient kindness is a small victory for the purposes of God. And when kindness is lived as a pattern, it is a surging wave of goodness in an unkind world.

Kindness is often the thin end of the wedge of the gospel of Christ. When you show consistent and genuine kindness to people who do not know God, they may open their hearts to God in a new way. Acts of kindness are the signposts of the goodness of God. When you do the opposite (live like a crank, a whiner, or a bigot), you're sure to push people further away from God. After all, who wants to worship a God who turns out ill-willed grumps as followers?

How are patterns of kindness established? Kindness is a choice, not a temperament; it is much more than a smile. In fact, some smiles are empty caves. Some smiles have a bite. I think the people who impact me the most with their kindness are not the naturally bright ones but the rough-and-tough kind of people, those who most people would not necessarily think of as kind (nor would they think it of themselves). When they show mercy, generosity, or goodwill, and when they do it as a pattern of their lives, the grace of God flows powerfully through them. Since kindness is a choice, not a temperament, there is hope for all of us.

And if you are one of those people who are naturally kind and considerate, enjoy the fact that you have a head start. You can be one of the bright spots in your office or in your family. You may be the one to reassure others of the radiance of God's created order, or you may be a pacesetter letting others know that kindness should be the norm in life, not the exception. Just remember that you don't have to smile through every circumstance. When it's other people's turn to do the smiling, let them.

PRAY THIS

Dear Father, your mercy is great; your generosity is ever-flowing. Thank you for showing us your kindness by sending your Son, Jesus. Now help me to recall your acts of kindness toward me in recent days. Amen.

FOR PERSONAL REFLECTION

1. What acts of kindness have made a deep impression on you?

2. What stands in the way of our showing kindness to each other?

3. What are the differences between superficial kindness and kindness that is "generosity, goodwill, mercy, and love toward people in distress"?

4. Who could use some kindness from you this week?

5. What can we do to set a habit, or pattern, of kindness in our lives?

THE GOOD LIFE

Goodness

9

Agray-haired grandfather in a powder-blue jacket walks haltingly through the cemetery at Normandy, on the north coast of France. He passes through the sea of clean white crosses and stars of David marking the resting places of hundreds of young men whose lives were cut off on D day; men who died so that multitudes could go on living in peaceable societies as parents and teachers, engineers and neighbors. The old man drops to his knees in front of the marker of the person who saved his life, tumbles into a moment of self-examination, and struggles to get out a plea to his wife, who is standing at his side: "Tell me I've lived a good life. . . . Tell me I'm a good man."

HAVE I LIVED A GOOD LIFE?

This scene from a popular film about World War II places goodness as the final tally, the supreme measure, of a person's life. The man wants to know whether his commander and all the others who paid the ultimate price made a difference—a difference of character—in the lives of others. If the recipients of such a great gift did not see life differently, did not live life differently, then what was it all for?

"Tell me I've lived a good life."

In one of Jesus' earthy stories a master (representing God) returns from a journey to find that one of his stewards had taken good care of his property. This steward's reward comes in these weighty words: "Well done, good and faithful servant! You have been faithful with a few things; I will put you in charge of many things. Come and share your master's happiness" (Matt. 25:23).

Well done and *good* are among the finest words any of us could ever hear in this life or at the door at the end of this life. Philosophers and theologians have used questions such as the following as baseline of our existence: What is a good life? What is goodness? How does a person become good?

But you don't need to read Plato to know that goodness is a pattern of life we deeply long for. Sometimes it may seem like we are more obsessed with looking good than with doing good, more obsessed with feeling good than with being good, but no matter how we put the words together, we are searching for the good. And anyone who has been pulled by the attractiveness of God, drawn by the gravitational force of the Divine, has been "called . . . by [God's] own glory and goodness" (2 Peter 1:3).

RIGHT, ATTRACTIVE, AND MORALLY EXCELLENT

When the Bible talks about the good, it means what is right, what is attractive, and what is morally excellent. Goodness, in other words, is more than not being bad.

Goodness is *rightness,* in the sense that the moving parts of a person's life are trued up. Things are made right between the person and God because God's forgiveness has begun to straighten out the crookedness. That then affects the other relationships of the person's life, giving him better order and better quality—if others will allow it.

Spiritual change is not always received with gratefulness. For the young husband whose wife has suddenly become "religious," the news of this change may be quite unwelcome. Despite the fact that his wife has experienced a dramatic transformation and a revolution of values, attitudes, and demeanor has begun, it upsets the apple cart.

The family had a certain spiritual posture, and now a pivotal member has become alive. Such conflict, however, can take nothing away from the pure rightness of a person's life turning decisively toward the eternal good.

Rightness is not first a matter of being correct; it is about being on the right side. It is better to be a mediocre soldier on God's side than an accomplished warrior on the other side.

Another meaning of goodness is *attractiveness*. People who live patterns of goodness are the people we want to be around. We are attracted to them because of the gratification that naturally comes from the good. They make us realize, "Yes, this is the way things are supposed to be." "That's what a good husband looks like." "She's a good girl." "He is a fine worker." Goodness makes us want to clap; it makes us smile and nod. Goodness gives us hope.

I believe this is why the spotlight shone so brightly on the brave survivors of the acts of terrorism on September 11, 2001. For no other reason than that the goodness of God shone brightly in her faith, every major television interviewer wanted to interview the wife of one man who bravely tried to stop the hijackers on a plane that crashed in Pennsylvania on that day. And there were the two young female Christian workers who were held captive in Afghanistan for months, praying their way through their dire situation. They described their ordeal with beaming faces and firm yet tender voices. A wife of one of the pilots whose plane was driven into the World Trade Center showed similar faith in the months following her tragic loss. What is this faith? It is goodness. And it is attractive beyond all measure. Upon discovering the sincerity of such people, interviewers who have no faith and who are used to probing at the cracks in a story become as wide-eyed and spiritually enthralled as any of us.

Goodness also means *moral excellence*. This has nothing to do with self-righteousness or spiritual superiority. Neither is moral excellence the once-in-a-century, legendary accomplishments of the Joan of Arcs of this world. We don't need only legends; we need good company. As God has planned it, goodness as moral excellence is to be as familiar as breakfast, lunch, and supper, not because it is easy but because it is simple. Moral excellence is not easy, because temptation and sin are always pulling us down like wet clothes on a drowning person. But it is simple in that faith—simple childlike faith—is the singular pathway to the good life.

THE GENESIS OF GOOD

Goodness is possible because examples of goodness are always only a few inches away from your face. This is the only reasonable way to understand Genesis 1.

In the very beginning of the story of the beginning, two words are repeated over and over: *God* and *good*. God created light "and saw that it was *good*." Then he created the dry ground and gathered the waters. Again, *"good."* Plants bearing seed and trees bearing food; God "saw that it was *good*." The sun and the moon. *Good*. Great creatures of the sea and every winged bird. *Good*. All the creatures that move along the ground. *Good*. And at the end of the creation, the final tally, the supreme measure, was this: "God saw all that he had made, and it was *very good*." Then God rested, and the good was simply . . . *good*. God gave us Genesis so we could step back, way back, from the whole of creation and see the theme of it all. That theme is goodness.

"Tell me I've lived a good life."

One might think that the heroism of D day would have caused every person involved to chart a sure course toward goodness. But such things are not automatic. When all is said and done, goodness is always a created thing, and there is only one Creator, only one who brings things into existence that wouldn't exist otherwise. The creatures God creates reflect an *inherent* goodness that is more basic than the issue of moral choices. To understand the possibility of human goodness, we need to pause and think through the declarations of the Creator when he beheld simple light, ordinary plants, creatures with fins, wings, or legs. Why did he declare them good? And what does their goodness have to do with the possibility of our goodness?

There is one common denominator here, and it is God himself. He is God the good: good because he is God, and God because he is good. Whenever God creates something, it is a good thing, because

God cannot bring into existence anything that is not right, attractive, and excellent.

This is the baseline and the genesis of goodness. I can understand why we spend as much time as we do in theology on the issues of corruption (the Fall) and restoration (redemption). But I sometimes wonder whether we have spent enough time considering creation and the two distinctive words of Genesis 1 and 2: *God* and *good*. To understand redemption, God's rescue of human beings, we have to understand what a human being was meant to be before the corruption set in. And we need to believe the biblical promise that redemption and sanctification will cause goodness to reemerge in the reality of our lives.

PRACTICAL GOODNESS

At a practical level, what needs to happen for any of us so that years from now we can say, "I think I've lived a good life"? Psalm 34 gives us some great guidance about this.

1. *Boldly seek ways to experience the goodness of God.* This is the point of verse 8: "Taste and see that the LORD is good." The psalmist is vividly telling us to take in the goodness of God. It's not a telescope we need to find the far-off goodness of God, not a textbook to read about the goodness of God, but daily faith that receives and consumes every good thing God offers. Tasting is different from casual glances and passing thoughts. Tasting means taking a risk, opening up, personally partaking. Tasting means being fully and personally engaged in worship. It means entering into some form of tiring, challenging, stretching service. You taste God's goodness when you open your mouth in worship and in private prayer.

In the Upper Room Jesus taught about the redemptive and sacrificial path his life was about to take, and then he passed the bread and said, "Take, eat," and then the cup, "Take, drink." It was as if he was saying, "I don't want these truths to bounce off your brains. I want you to open your very selves, to take and consume what I offer. I want to leave a taste in your mouth and a vivid memory in your mind."

2. *Consume God's Word.* The metaphor of taste is amplified in all the passages where God says that his Word is to be taken so deeply into our lives that we profoundly experience its goodness. God's Word is sweet to the taste, sweeter than honey (Ps. 119:103). Ezekiel ate a scroll (by God's command) that tasted as sweet as honey (Ezek. 3:3), as did John in the Apocalypse (Rev. 10:10). First Peter 2:2–3 says, "Like newborn babies, crave pure spiritual milk, so that by it you may grow up in your salvation, now that you have tasted that the Lord is good." For our day the application is simple: take God's Word in, and take time to meditate on it. Reading without rumination is like gulping down a meal. The food disappears, but it does not please and it does not nourish in the same way.

3. *Guard your own words.* Psalm 34 says, "Whoever of you loves life and desires to see many good days, keep your tongue from evil and your lips from speaking lies" (vv. 12–13). One of the distinguishing features of a good life is that the tongue is used for blessing instead of cursing (James 3:9–12) and for giving life instead of destroying life (Prov. 18:21). Good words, like goodness itself, are distinguished by rightness, attractiveness, and moral excellence. We can filter our speech by first asking: Is it correct? Is it beneficial? Is it morally excellent?

4. *Do whatever you can to seek peace.* Psalm 34 goes on to say, "Turn from evil and do good; seek peace and pursue it" (v. 14). When we taste and see that the Lord is good, we are shown possibilities beyond our imagining. The climax of the Bible is a picture of a great wedding banquet, the ultimate feast, the final satiation of all hunger, the taste beyond all tastes. But God wants us to hunger for goodness even now. The good life includes:

- valuing peace so much that you are willing to swallow your pride and say you're sorry
- taking positions as a citizen that are for the common good, not just your own good
- responding, not just reacting
- expending yourself (your time, talents, and treasures) in the pursuit of peace in your relationships, your community, and the world

PRAY THIS

God, create something in my life today. Put in a new thought —right from you. Plant a fresh motive in my heart. Take your view of the people around me and impress it on my mind. Create in me a clean heart, O God. For I know that anything you create has to be good, even if it gets mixed up with the ugly parts of my own soul. You are good; you will always be good. I want to live a good life. I want other people to see that you are still creating. Please do in my life what only you can do. In Christ's name, Amen.

FOR PERSONAL REFLECTION

1. Think about some of the common expressions we use when speaking of others, such as "She's a good wife," "He's a good father," "He's a good boy," "She's a very good friend." What do we mean when we use such expressions?

2. Read the creation story in Genesis 1. Why would things like light, trees, and birds be called "good"?

3. If you overheard someone talking about you, saying, "He is a good . . . ," what would you hope would be the next words out of that person's mouth? Why?

4. One day someone addressed Jesus as "good teacher," and Jesus said, "No one is good—except God alone," which was his way of saying, "Don't use the word *good* unless you really appreciate what it means." In what ways do we use the word *good* somewhat flippantly?

5. What do you hope God might create in you in the days to come?

DARE TO TRUST
Faithfulness

10

He knew that somebody up there was looking for him. He had faith, not just wishful thinking. And the reason he could have faith is because of the faithfulness of the multitude of men and women who were his backup, who wouldn't let a downed F-16 pilot be abandoned.

Captain Scott O'Grady had been on the ground in Bosnia for six days already. After his plane was crippled by antiaircraft fire, he ejected and parachuted into a hostile landscape. Amazingly, he eluded capture, sometimes with his face buried in the ground as he heard the voices of the soldiers walking just yards from where he was lying. At night he moved. He survived by drinking rainwater from leaves and by wringing water out of his socks.

And then on the sixth day after O'Grady's disappearance, one of his buddies flying in the search mission heard the crackling sound of O'Grady's radio. Tears filled the pilot's eyes as he struggled to concentrate on flying his plane. The strategists went to work, and a Marine rescue team was assembled on the deck of the USS *Kearsarge* assault ship amidst the noise of chopping helicopter rotors and screaming jet engines. Then they took off: two AH1 Super Cobra attack helicopters to lead the way, two gigantic CH53E Super Stallion heli-copters, and four AV8B Harrier strike aircraft. Forty support aircraft stood by. The rescue team swooped low across the countryside, snatched up the downed pilot, and within a couple of hours Scott O'Grady was safe on the *Kearsarge* in the Adriatic Sea.

This is a picture of faithfulness. One man was able to trust in and rely on other people because he knew their values, their purpose, their priorities, and their readiness to fly in the face of danger. He waited for his rescuers, knowing he would not give up on them because they would not give up on him.

QUIT OR TRUST

Sometimes in life we face this kind of choice: Quit or trust. If you are willing to trust, you will need someone nearby who is trustworthy.

Faithfulness is an indispensable pattern of character, because none of us can live without trusting someone else. You trust the anes-thesiologist and the surgeon when you undergo an operation; you trust the airline pilot, control tower personnel, and jet mechanics when you settle into your seat on an airliner; you trust your teach-ers to assist you in becoming an educated person.

I've had the privilege of knowing many faithful people—not flaw-less people, but fundamentally reliable people. I've been married to one of them for the past twenty-seven years. It is a blessing I try not to take for granted. My wife's faithfulness to me goes beyond what I deserve. Trusting Ingrid takes no conscious effort on my part, because her faithful spirit makes it easy. I know that she does not lie to me, she does not flatter me, she does not expect unreasonable things from me. She expects me to be and to do what God wants—not more, not less. She challenges me when I need challenging and comforts me when I need comforting. Most important of all, she is not faithful to me because of me, but because of God. Long before I met Ingrid as a teenager, God was shaping her heart in such a way that she longed for integrity with God. So I suppose if I asked her, "Why are you so faithful to me?" a right answer would be, "It's because of God, silly, not you."

TRUST VIOLATED

Sometimes trust is violated. You have faith in somebody who becomes unfaithful, or perhaps that person never was faithful in the first place. Sometimes we are disappointed by others and they don't even know it. They're oblivious to the reality that you were counting on them, and they go on their merry way not knowing that they left you stranded. Oftentimes the explanation for unfaithfulness is just bald-faced self-interest.

Harder still is the reality that we fail others. No human being is trustworthy and reliable all the time in every way. So it is inevitable that as a part of the rhythm of life we will have to apologize to friends, family, and acquaintances. We'll have to say, "I know you were counting on me, and I know I didn't live up to your trust." If you have failed someone in a devastating way, you can ask for forgiveness, but you can't expect trust until you've demonstrated your trustworthiness over an appropriate length of time.

BLOCK BY BLOCK

Faithfulness only works as a pattern. There is no such thing as instant trust. Reliability is a quality of character that is built progressively over time. Faithfulness as a quality of marriage, for instance, emerges from a history of trustworthy exchanges. Like building a house block by block, board by board, there comes a time when you step back and start calling it a house. It may not be complete yet, but it has the shape of a house, the rooms are roughed in, and you can imagine living in it. But you don't think that way in the early days. The foundation may be there, a few boards may be visible, but the house is still more theory than fact.

It's a tremendous thing when people can give each other the benefit of the doubt, relying on each other step by step until trust is built up into trustworthiness and faith matures into faithfulness.

If there is any hope for faithfulness, it will come only from God. Faithfulness is at the core of God's character. The Bible is exuberant about the faithfulness of God. "For the LORD is good and his love endures forever; his faithfulness continues through all generations" (Ps. 100:5). "For great is your love, higher than the heavens; your faithfulness reaches to the skies" (Ps. 108:4). "The Lord is faithful, and he will strengthen and protect you from the evil one" (2 Thess. 3:3). A man who had seen the worst kind of affliction could still say, "Because of the LORD's great love we are not consumed, for his compassions never fail. They are new every morning; great is your faithfulness" (Lam. 3:22–23).

It's no wonder the Bible encourages us to build the pattern of faithfulness in our own lives. "Let love and *faithfulness* never leave you; bind them around your neck, write them on the tablet of your heart" (Prov. 3:3, emphasis added). Faithfulness is the bedrock of our relationship with God, who doesn't ask us to have faith in him simply as a theory. He asks us to have faith because he is faithful. And so it is with other relationships. The only way of standing in a relationship is trust, and the only thing you can stand on is the trustworthiness of the other person.

Scott O'Grady was not the only person downed behind enemy lines. We are all in danger. The world can be a benevolent place and it can be hostile territory. There is hope for every one of us because God's faithfulness "reaches to the skies." And it is likely that God wants to use you as part of the rescue team sent to retrieve others who are hoping against hope to find somebody, somewhere, they can really trust.

FAITHFUL AND TRUE

The book of Revelation presents an image of Jesus that should be burned into our minds. A rider on a mighty white horse. Eyes of blazing fire, wearing many crowns, robe dipped in blood. He is called the Word of God. He is also called King of Kings and Lord of Lords. Armies follow him, multitudes of riders dressed in fine white linen, all of whom ride white horses. It is the ultimate picture of triumph and sheer power. This vision begins with the words: "I saw heaven standing open and there before me was a white horse, whose rider is called Faithful and True" (Rev. 19:11).

Faithful and True. All of Jesus' power, all of his truth, his love, and his majesty would mean nothing if he was not faithful. Because he is faithful—utterly and completely faithful—faith in him can be for the first and easiest act of the day and the last thought of the evening.

PRAY THIS

Thank you, Lord, for your great faithfulness. I believe, but I need you to help me with my unbelief. Surely I am unaware of many of the ways you have been faithful to me. Open my eyes so that I don't miss your acts of faithfulness.

Help me to be a person of faithfulness. Teach me through my failures, but help me to move beyond regret. Help me this week to do and to say things that are worthy of the trust of others. Don't let me avoid the burden of carrying the trust of others.

Amen.

FOR PERSONAL REFLECTION

1. Do a verse-by-verse study of the Scripture passages cited in this chapter. Better yet, use a concordance to look up the fifty or sixty Bible passages that use the word *faithfulness* and read each passage. What do these passages tell us about how we can be faithful to each other?

2. It is easy for us to take the faithfulness of God for granted. How would your life be different if God were not faithful?

3. If you were to declare that you want everybody around you to know you as a faithful person and to benefit from goodwilled, steady commitment on your part, what would you need to do differently in the weeks and months to come?

4. When have you failed to be reliable? What are your regrets?

5. In what specific ways would you like to see a growth of faithfulness in your own life in the months to come?

SECRET STRENGTH
Gentleness

11

I have to admit, I had little enthusiasm for writing on the theme of gentleness. It's not for lack of interest. Certainly we'd all agree that the soft touch is nice once in a while. But gentleness hardly seems a riveting theme. Awfully tame, docile, maybe even weak.

But I realize that I am at fault for underestimating the theme of gentleness. We live in an age when power gets the attention, conflict piques our interest, blood sells newspapers, and push and pull are the ways people move or are moved.

It is a world of friction.

Human beings can be destructively harsh. We are often severe with each other, sometimes brutal. Rudeness, disrespect, angry outbursts, and other primitive behavior are the uncivilized norms of modern civilization. We may not wear the rough clothing of barbarians of the past, but our treatment of each other is often just as barbaric.

And that is why we need gentleness.

THE STRENGTH OF GENTLENESS

Gentleness is the discipline of being consistently courteous with others. It is motivated by attitudes of humility and love. Gentleness is not weakness. Only a very strong person can choose to be composed and civil. We are strongest when we are gentle. We are weak when we crash through life like the proverbial bull in a china shop. Pushiness and unchecked aggressiveness are the easy ways to respond. The public may applaud the person who gets to the top by stepping on others, but who wants to marry that person?

Gentleness is not just passive submission. Letting other people walk all over you is not the gift of a gentle spirit; it is just getting stepped on. Gentleness is the response that says, "Please remove your shoe from my back. It does not belong there. And it does neither of us any good for it to remain there."

Gentleness is sometimes the deliberate choice to sacrifice. When we, with God's help, choose not to pay back evil for evil, choose not to return a harsh word with one harsher, choose not to calculate how we can make someone pay for what he has done to us, that is gentleness. It may seem like gentleness puts us into a deficit on the balance sheet of life. How, after all, can we be respectable if we don't even the score once in a while? But the fact of the matter is, no one in heaven is keeping score, so no one on earth should either. The world is a competitive place, and we compare ourselves all the time, but in truth, life itself is not a competition. You and I can afford to be gentle, even self-sacrificially, because real civility is an accomplishment that is as good as gold.

RESPONDING TO THE WORLD AROUND YOU

Gentleness has to be a pattern. Rare and passing acts of gentleness do not produce civility; they only confuse others. If a dog licks your extended hand three times out of ten and bites it the other seven times, the friendly licks don't mean much. So it is with us. We need God to develop in us a pattern of gentleness, because only God can put a spirit of gentleness into us so that we can develop a consistent habit of considerate, moderate responses to the people and the events of our lives.

How can we develop a pattern of gentleness? Here are some suggestions.

1. *Ask God to moderate your responses to others.* Many of our rude moments come when we react instead of respond. The Bible says to be "slow to speak and slow to become angry" (James 1:19) because impulsivity so easily gets us into trouble. If we were perfect creatures, we could fling open the door of our souls, and all that would come out would be goodness. As it is, we have to be doorkeepers and control our tongues, with God's help. "A gentle answer turns away wrath, but a harsh word stirs up anger" (Prov. 15:1).

2. *See gentleness as the way to express other character patterns.* Love, patience, kindness, faithfulness, and self-control are passed on through the firm mildness of gentleness. "Be completely humble and gentle; be patient, bearing with one another in love" (Eph. 4:2). A parent expresses patience, for instance, with the unhurried and gentle word, not a shout. When we want to show kindness to someone, we usually begin with a gentle tone of voice. Many fathers whom I've talked to say that of all the fruit of the Spirit, they most need to work on self-control and gentleness (and they say they sincerely wish their own fathers had had more of both).

3. *Focus on the gentleness with which God has treated all of us.* "Therefore, as God's chosen people, holy and dearly loved, clothe yourselves with compassion, kindness, humility, gentleness and patience" (Col. 3:12). I think the Israelites had a better sense of this. They knew God to be mighty and powerful and were probably amazed with each encounter with God that his greatness did not crush them.

4. *Pay attention to those who speak with gentleness.* I recently attended a symposium with about twenty-five other Christian leaders to discuss spiritual transformation. Many profound thoughts were shared around the table. But about halfway through the day I realized that the comments I found to be most helpful and most intriguing were coming from people

whose voices were so gentle that you had to strain to hear what they were saying. They spoke sparingly and showed no need to impress anybody else. Granted, God speaks through people of all kinds of different voices. He uses blasters and he uses whisperers. I tend toward the verbose and loud end of the spectrum, though I am continually seeking self-control on this issue. My point is simply this: think of how much we miss when we pay attention only to the loudest voices in the room.

5. *Appreciate the power and strategic importance of gentleness.* Ask yourself this: If you were not a believer and someone approached you to convince you of the truth of the gospel of Christ, would you be more likely to believe a bombastic, over-bearing presentation or one that respects you as a thinking, independent person? "Let your gentleness be evident to all. The Lord is near" (Phil. 4:5). "In your hearts set apart Christ as Lord. Always be prepared to give an answer to everyone who asks you to give the reason for the hope that you have. But do this with gentleness and respect" (1 Peter 3:15).

6. *Learn from the gentleness of Jesus.* "Take my yoke upon you and learn from me, for I am gentle and humble in heart, and you will find rest for your souls" (Matt. 11:29).

The gentleness of Jesus is one of the keys to understanding who he is; it is also one of the most misunderstood of his characteristics. Some have dismissed Jesus because of his gentleness. They have viewed him as a naive leader of a pitiful band of followers who scattered after he fell victim to those who had real power. But none of Jesus' murderers inspired a world movement that has changed the lives of millions of people.

Others who respect Jesus have taken comfort in his gentleness but exaggerate it to the point that Jesus becomes merely a tame image, a quaint curiosity. A soft glowing picture to be hung on a wall. A nice memory. A useful set of quotes. But Jesus' brand of gentleness is anything but tame. He sacrificed himself for others time and again, but he never let anyone take advantage of him. He suffered the insufferable pettiness and self-interest of his enemies and his friends, but he never lost any of his dignity. His words were brief and they were gentle, but they exploded like fireworks in the minds of his listeners.

Jesus is the most powerful ruler the world has ever known, yet look at what kind of king he is: "Your king comes to you, *gentle* and riding on a donkey" (Matt. 21:5, emphasis added).

PRACTICE THIS

During the week as you interact with others you know and don't know, try to take twice as much time as you normally would in responding to them. Use this pause to think, "What is the next thing I can say that will add civility to this interaction?"

FOR PERSONAL REFLECTION

1. Talk about some examples of when you have seen someone respond gently in a dicey situation. How did gentleness affect the situation?

2. In what kinds of situations is it easy to have a gentle response? When is it difficult?

3. Discuss what you find out about gentleness in some or all of the following biblical passages:

Deuteronomy 28:54, 56	1 Corinthians 4:21
2 Samuel 18:5	2 Corinthians 10:1
1 Kings 19:12	Ephesians 4:2
Job 41:3	Philippians 4:5
Proverbs 15:1	Colossians 3:12
Proverbs 25:15	1 Thessalonians 2:7
Zechariah 9:9	1 Timothy 6:11
Matthew 11:29	1 Peter 3:4, 15
Matthew 21:5	

TAMING DIONYSUS
Self-Control

12

He was the bad boy of the Greek gods. He was good to those who treated him well but brought madness to others. He was the god of wine and vegetation and was the inspiration behind the spring fertility rites—riotous, boisterous, drunken festivals called the Bacchanalia, after his Roman name, Bacchus. The Greeks called him Dionysus.

Apollo, on the other hand, was the god of light and truth, a perfect picture of restraint and discipline. This archer was a straight shooter and stood for logical order and complete sobriety.

The stories of myth are the way peoples have tried to understand their own behavior. In the last hundred years or so, modern people have debated in literature and philosophy whether it's better to be a Dionysus or an Apollo. A Dionysus may be unpredictable, savage, and driven by pleasure, but is the icy restraint and passionless control of an Apollo really a better alternative? Many modern stories portray one character who is alive in the middle of a dead community, someone who wears red boldly, who dips into the untamed energy and creativity that is in the spirit of Dionysus. The modern world is fascinated with the primitive and sometimes seems to believe that baser may be better.

But there is a better alternative than either Dionysus or Apollo. It is possible to be alive with instinct, creativity, and enjoyment and to be self-controlled at the same time.

WHO CAN CONTROL THE SELF?

Self-control is the last word used in that list the Bible calls "the fruit of the Spirit." It is a pattern of character that keeps us from being self-destructively out of control. To put it positively, self-control is the stability that comes from sober self-awareness and intentional choice. It is what we need to prevent us from speaking rash and hurtful words, from indulging in self-destructive excess, and from making sexual advances that are out of bounds.

Now, it would be a mistake to think that the term *self-control* means that we can, with ease, always direct our impulses and actions.

Christian faith teaches that we are not capable of controlling ourselves with our own willpower or genius. If self-control is possible, it is only because God has trained us to have that control. It is called self-control because the pattern is produced in the self, but it is not self-generated.

Now this is a repugnant idea for people who are placing their bets on their ability to be the captain of their own souls. And of course, God allows people to pursue that option, as ill-fated as it is. You can steer your own ship, but do you really feel up to taking on the high seas of life all by yourself?

CONTROLLING THE UNCONTROLLABLE

The Bible says that when it comes to the tongue (our speech), we are dealing with a wild thing in need of direction: "All kinds of animals, birds, reptiles and creatures of the sea are being tamed and have been tamed by man, but no man can tame the tongue. It is a restless evil, full of deadly poison. With the tongue we praise our Lord and Father, and with it we curse men, who have been made in

God's likeness. Out of the same mouth come praise and cursing. My brothers, this should not be" (James 3:7–10).

How many times have you said something you wish you could take back? If you sometimes wonder, "Why don't I know better than that? How could I have said something so rash, so unwise?" then join the club. If we're honest, we'll admit that "reckless words pierce like a sword, but the tongue of the wise brings healing" (Prov. 12:18).

There are many reasons we need self-control. Self-control is necessary so that sexual relationships are a bond of serious covenantal commitments in marriage, not the prowling behavior of a species looking for serial mating. We need self-control so that we don't abuse our own bodies by absorbing damaging substances or by immorality or by sheer neglect. Since the body is "a temple of the Holy Spirit" (1 Cor. 6:19), we have an opportunity to show respect for God by exercising control in how we care for his dwelling place. "Therefore honor God with your body" (1 Cor. 6:20).

Self-control is the inner structure and discipline we need to make good daily decisions about our lifestyles. How much television is helpful and reasonable? What do I need to do to get a good night's rest? How can I make sure I don't forget the appointments and commitments I have made? What kind of work should I commit to doing?

MASTER OF THE MASTER OF THE SELF

The Greek word for self-control literally means "mastery of the self." When it comes to self-control, we greatly need God's help; only God can be the Master of the master of the self. Some of us need to say to him, "I am a Dionysus. I am completely out of control. And my head is spinning so fast I don't know which way to turn to get my bearings." Others need to say, "God, I'm an Apollo. I'm so rigid with self-imposed self-control that nobody wants to be around me. I'm wound so tightly that I'm afraid I'm going to snap someday. I'm so sharp-edged that people get cut by just being around me. I need to discover your control in my life, not my own stilted and fragile self-righteousness."

Here are some steps we can take to adopt the kind of pattern the Bible describes as genuine life-giving self-control.

1. *Begin with faith.* A trust relationship with God is the way we can know him as our loving Father and beneficent Master. Faith and love prevent us from thinking of God as an all-powerful referee just waiting to blow the whistle on our next violation. That is not the kind of control he exercises. Faith is freedom. It liberates us from the burden of having to find all our self-control from within. It snatches from us all pride and pretence about how wonderfully disciplined we are. Faith makes boasting sound just silly.

2. *Fill faith with knowledge.* Begin with childlike faith, but don't stop there. God's truth can move into our minds like a continually flowing stream, and that truth can be a living, controlling influence. Self-control works best when there is an ever-maturing self-understanding. In lower stages we come to understand that we have dangerous impulses that we need to control (for example, realizing you're susceptible to chemical dependency, gambling, adultery, pornography, or gossip). At a higher level, spiritually sound knowledge brings understanding about *why* we turn to such impulses (for example, you may understand that you are suppressing pain, rebelling against your parents, looking for acceptance, or filling up loneliness). Then, by God's grace, comes some understanding of how to intervene and break the rhythm of misbehavior. And then we seek to understand how good patterns can replace our bad patterns.

3. *Ask God to shape your desires.* If we want to have self-control, we have to want the qualities we're aiming at. That may seem to be obvious, but the story can be told many times over of how we can hate ourselves in the morning for acting like Dionysus, but as the day wanes and the darkness approaches, we don't really know what other role to take. Our prayer needs to go way beyond "Lord, I truly regret using the members of my body to sin once again." Our prayer must be "Lord, work

in the deepest and hidden part of my heart where my impulses are coming from, and shape them into instincts that are wholesome and good."

4. *Admit to God and, as appropriate, to others just where you feel out of control in your life.* Don't pretend here. Don't try to be an Apollo. Follow the pattern of the apostle Paul—even Paul!—who told us that we have the treasure of God in jars of clay. Remember that Jesus said that the truly righteous person is not one who gloats over his spiritual accomplishments but is the person who "would not even look up to heaven, but beat his breast and said, 'God, have mercy on me, a sinner'" (Luke 18:13). If you've never stopped and meditated on this saying, it's time to do so. Jesus is giving us permission to pray even when we don't know what to pray because we don't understand God's ways and we're astounded by our own waywardness.

5. *Commit to the patterns of devotion that train us in the disciplines that keep us in control* (themes in part 3 of this book).

6. *Don't be idle.* Lack of spiritual movement is a dangerous way to live. It makes us vulnerable to controlling forces that others may try to exert on us. Spending long hours at church isn't going to guarantee that you will be more holy for having been there. But being active in the community of Christ is a far better option than hanging out in places where you know you are playing with fire and testing self-control beyond what is wise. If you want to have self-control, eschew situations with stimuli that assault you where you are weakest.

Some of the people who encourage me the most are those who have struggled for a very long time with some out-of-control behavior in their lives and have gradually appropriated the power of God to master the master of the self. Several men I knew in college who were the typical fraternity boys, whose wild weekends started on Thursday and who were as close as you can get to Dionysus in blue jeans, are now members in the church where I serve. They have a truly dramatic view of the stages of their lives. They see where they were twenty-five years ago and know they will *never* go back. It was not with pride of self that they got their act together, because they found they couldn't do it on their own. They are the people who learned the hard way that Dionysus can't really be tamed; he must be transformed.

MORE THAN VIRTUES

I mentioned in chapter 3 the couple with the troubled marriage who, upon hearing about love, joy, peace, patience, kindness, goodness, gentleness, faithfulness, and self-control, said, "If we had those things, there's nothing else we would ask for." Indeed, how could any of us ask for more?

But if we just left it at that, this list would be like the many catalogs of virtues that high-minded philosophers have come up with throughout the ages (although they would not usually include the virtues of grace, like love, kindness, gentleness, and self-control). The difference between philosophy and the Christian faith is that Scripture doesn't just give us a set of character specifications with the assumption that we will try our hardest to achieve them. Christian faith asserts that fractured human nature needs nothing less than a supernatural process of transformation.

In part 3 of this book we will examine the patterns of Christian lifestyle—prayer, worship, Scripture reading, meditation, service, solitude—that keep us under the continual influence of the Spirit of God. There is no use longing for the fruit of the Spirit unless we are willing to live the life of the Spirit through faith. What greater assurance can we have that a God-filled life is possible than that we are offered "the fullness of the Spirit" who indwells believers?

PRACTICE THIS

At the end of each day this week ask God to help you review where you made good choices and where you lacked self-control. Begin the next day by asking God for his help in new ways. Think carefully about whether you could or should ask somebody else to pray for you and to help you keep track of how things are going for you.

FOR PERSONAL REFLECTION

1. In what areas of our lives is self-control most important (that is, those areas where lack of self-control can be devastating)?

2. Discuss what you learn about self-control in the following passages: Proverbs 25:28; Acts 24:25; 1 Corinthians 7:5; 2 Timothy 3:3; 2 Peter 1:6.

3. How can you pray for God's control in your life in a new way?

4. Who do you know who needs your prayers to find a degree of self-control in his or her life?

PART THREE

DEVOTION PATTERNS

DEVOTED

13

In the previous section of this book we explored the captivating description of God-filled character: love, joy, peace, patience, kindness, goodness, gentleness, faithfulness, and self-control. It is too weak to describe these qualities as character traits, because they are not merely superficial descriptions of contours but the substance of personhood. And they are not exactly virtues, by which we usually mean descriptions of quality. The fruit of the Spirit are to be the very shape and substance of personhood; they are the pattern of what a girl, boy, man, or woman is to become.

But being the cracked clay creatures that we are and living in this both glorious and utterly corrupted world, we need a work of God to do the shaping.

I remember as a college student standing in a church in Rome called San Pietro in Vincoli, marveling at a striking statue of Moses that had been liberated from a colossal marble block by Michelangelo 450 years ago. Like other Renaissance sculpture, the human figure of Moses seems almost alive. His powerful arms and legs bulge, showing fine lines and rippled surfaces. His face is set with determination, framed by locks of hair and a beard that look like anything but stone. How did he see that shape in the stone? Michelangelo, who wanted to be known as a sculptor, not a painter, believed that he was drawing something out that was inherent in the stone rather than imposing something on it. "The best of artists has no conception that the marble alone does not contain within itself."

One day someone asked Michelangelo how he was able to take a block of marble and sculpt it into a stunning statue that seemed to be alive. His reply? "I saw the angel in the marble and I carved until I set him free." Now if an Italian sculptor can do that with a block of cold, dead stone, imagine what God can do with a living, breathing, sentient, intelligent, spiritual being whom he created in the first place. God can do it, and he does do it.

God has called us to a life of the Spirit in which we engage in a set of behaviors, which we will call "devotion patterns" in the chapters that follow. No magic here. And no mechanical process either. Devotion patterns are the natural way for spiritual beings to live, as natural as breathing and eating, which we do without conscious thought of utilitarian necessity. So it must be with patterns of devotion. We will know we are living a God-filled life as we experience him filling out our prayers, filling us in worship, emptying us, and filling us again through godly service.

But first, a warning and a disclaimer. Unlike breathing and eating, devotion is a value and an appetite continually threatened by our own fleshly nature and by the dark spiritual forces at work in the world. A battle is going on in every soul and for every soul. The good things of God do not rise up as casually as a colorful hot-air balloon on a Sunday afternoon. Any hope we have of a genuinely upward motion of life comes only through the power of resurrection.

○ ○ ○

Sailors have two main opponents: dead calm and storms. Too little wind and too much.

The emptiness we have inside without God is sometimes like the dead calm that sailors find near the equator, which leaves them with no wind to fill their sails. Those frustrating regions are called the doldrums, which is why we use this lazy-sounding word for dull listlessness.

More often spiritual emptiness is like a vacuum. This kind of empty space wants to pull something in. Remember what you were taught in science class? "Nature abhors a vacuum." I remember thinking, "What an odd expression that is, almost personifying emptiness itself." But the phrase is so vivid I never forgot it. Nature abhors a vacuum. Emptiness longs to fill itself with something.

One sultry day I was walking across a parking lot to my car when I noticed in the distance a gray funnel in the sky, reaching down and waving across the earth. For a split second I experienced an emotionless sense of recognition: "Oh, yes, I know what that is. I've seen pictures of them. How wonderful to see one in person!" But then a sense of dread rose up from the bottom of my abdomen until it reached my head. I looked back at the store I had just exited, a metal shed of a building, and realized that I didn't want to be inside a shredded warehouse if the tornado took it apart. So I got in my car and drove on the highway (at something more than the speed limit) in the opposite direction of the tornado. Seeing it in the rearview mirrors was reassuring, except when I looked at the mirror with the words: "Objects are larger than they appear in mirror."

What makes a tornado so terrifying? It is a vacuum. The swirling winds create a powerful emptiness that sucks in anything in its path, and it is all that random stuff sucked in—dirt and boards and paper and leaves and housing insulation—that makes a cyclone so ominously visible.

Nature abhors a vacuum. We will draw into our lives something to fill the spiritual emptiness that is there. Longing will attach itself to something or someone.

WHAT WILL FILL THE VACUUM?

This is where devotion comes in. Devotion is the conscious commitment to doing those things that will fill our lives with what is good and right. We are not impersonal vacuums. We were designed to be filled by the God who created us. That is how love, joy, peace, patience, kindness, goodness, gentleness, faithfulness, and self-control become the shape of our character.

In its simplest form, devotion means dedication. So one person may be devoted to auto restoration or fly fishing or bowling. Someone else may be devoted to collecting music or dog breeding. We can be grateful for the cardiac surgeon who doesn't take the profession halfheartedly but is devoted to the highest level of competence when he or she takes people's hearts apart and puts them back together.

More often, however, we use the word *devotion* to refer to commitments that go well beyond our vocations or avocations. And for good reason.

Devotion runs deep in the human heart. It is about commitments that arise out of our strongest affections and our deepest longings. It is an essentially spiritual motion in the direction of God.

Devotion patterns are those habits we develop over time that will bring our longing right to God himself. Such habits include prayer, worship, and reading and studying Scripture. They are the spiritual exercises and habits of devotion that the first Christians knew would make them strong. "They devoted themselves to the apostles' teaching and to the fellowship, to the breaking of bread and to prayer" (Acts 2:42). These are some of the themes that we will now be exploring.

FORMATION AND TRANSFORMATION

Spiritual formation is the progressive patterning of a person's inner and outer life according to the image of Christ through intentional means of spiritual growth. Patterns or habits of devotion are these intentional means. Some people call them spiritual disciplines.

Whatever you call them, the underlying principle is that the life of soul and spirit, as it affects the life of the body, is supposed to have a certain form to it. There is something to be learned from the fact that the Bible nowhere gives an exact to-do list for the life of faith but instead sees it as a dynamic interaction between us and God. Just as from infancy to adulthood our bodies grow not only bigger but into a more defined form, so our spiritual lives are supposed to be shaped into a particular form by the hand of God. Call it transformation or formation or being conformed to the image of Christ, it is the way

God takes our twisted and bent selves and brings them into a form or shape that is like the perfect human nature of Christ.

The Bible teaches that God uses many forces to shape us, usually over a considerable length of time. That's how all growing things in the kingdom of God develop.

Of course, God has his own timetable on such matters. One of the most moving moments in our church in recent years was the baptism of Olga—at age one hundred. She was born before World War I and before the Russian Revolution, but she was reborn at the age of ninety-eight. Now this was no transfer of church membership, no switching of personal spiritual styles. Olga was a true nonbeliever for all those years. She was cantankerous, mean-spirited, and unhappy her whole life. She recalls growing up envying the loving affection that other children received from their parents. When Olga was ninety-eight years old God came to her. One night she knew that Jesus Christ was calling her to faith in him. Now she has told thousands of people how in the weeks and months that followed that night, peace and joy came over her that she had never known in her whole life. She gained confidence and a sense of purpose. And she has been preaching in the nursing home where she resides.

This is transformation. Patterns of devotion will help Olga in her remaining days on earth, but frankly, she doesn't have time to wait for the ten-year spiritual-formation program. The Holy Spirit touched her quickly, deeply, and effectively. I've heard experts say that people do not change fundamentally after age twenty. Don't try to tell Olga that.

Only spiritual creatures can be devoted. We know about God and long for him to fill our lives because we were made in his image. This is the exclusive prerogative of sons and daughters of Adam and Eve. You will never go downstairs early in the morning and find your dog or cat having devotions. No one has ever found in the forest a religious shrine constructed by the animals, nor the personal spiritual journals of a jungle animal. The ability to be truly devoted is the privilege and native ability of humanity. (So what does it say about us when sometimes our dogs and cats are more devoted to us than we are to God?)

KNOW YOUR MOTIVES

Before even beginning to talk about the specific devotion patterns, however, we need to pause and think through our motives. Actions of devotion with the wrong motives are extremely dangerous. Attempting any one of the following is all it takes to turn devotion into something either powerless or reckless.

1. *Trying to impress God.* Our devotion will never be impressive to God. Devotion is supposed to be as natural to the spirit as breathing is to the body. If a child tried to show off to an adult about how well he was breathing, the adult might be amused but would not be impressed. God wants us as friends and sons and daughters, not performers.

2. *Trying to impress others.* We could try to gain points with some people with public piety, but just a drop of pride will begin to poison our spiritual lives. That is why Jesus insisted so absolutely that we do "acts of righteousness" (like praying and making our offerings) in secret. The actor (which is the meaning of the word *hypocrite*) plays to the public and receives the appropriate reward—applause on earth—but no reward, only silence, from heaven (Matt. 6:1–4).

3. *Trying to impress yourself.* You won't convince yourself anyway, so why try?

4. *Trying to make yourself feel better about yourself.* It isn't wrong to want to feel right with God. But we also need to know as deeply as we know anything else that our relationship with God begins and ends with his loving grace and our openness to him through faith. Prayers do not take away sin; God does. Bible reading is not the knowledge of God; it is the way we get knowledge of God. Acts of worship do not give us joy, but they open us to the movement of God's Spirit, which does result in joy and, for that matter, brokenness, illumination, and affection.

5. *Trying to have occasional bursts of devotion.* Devotion is not a matter of going to one spectacular conference a year or of going to church at Christmas and Easter. You can't build a

marriage by going out for your anniversary each year and being indifferent toward your spouse the other 364 days of the year. Devotion is the accumulating effect of many small acts. It is a rhythm in the background that keeps us in step with God.

So then, what is devotion?

DEVOTION IS LOVE

To put it positively: devotion is love. The motive behind prayer and worship and all the rest has to be at its start and at its end an affectionate longing to know God better. What will move us in that direction? The inspiration, naturally, is God's abundant love for us. This is how one of the German Pietists of the seventeenth century, Count Zinzendorf, put it: "Lord, when my eye confronts my heart, and I realize that you have filled my heart with your love, I am breathless with amazement. Once my heart was so small in its vision, so narrow in its compassion, so weak in its zeal for truth. Then you chose to enter my heart, and now in my heart I can see you, I can love all your people, and I have courage to proclaim the truth of your gospel to anyone and everyone. Like wax before a fire, my heart has melted under the heat of your love."

We can be very glad that we don't need to figure this out on our own. We can follow the lead of others who are wiser than we are. As the apostle Paul put it, "Join with others in following my example, brothers, and take note of those who live according to the pattern we gave you" (Phil. 3:17).

PRAY THIS

Dear Lord, I know I don't understand my heart as much as you do. I want to know if there is anything I'm devoted to that is hurting my relationship with you. I want to even out the unevenness of my devotion to you. Please help me to be drawn by your love. Make my devotion to you as natural as breathing. Protect me from clumsy and self-conscious acts that are empty. Help me when I'm discouraged about my relationship with you and humble me if I have any self-importance about it. Grant me a simple and pure affection for you. In Christ's name, Amen.

FOR PERSONAL REFLECTION

1. How have you been disappointed in seeking a devotion to God?
2. What are some personal reasons that you would like to develop and deepen devotion as the simple and natural pulse of your life?
3. Whom do you know who has been a good example of devotion to God?
4. What kinds of examples of devotion to God have troubled you or made you leery?

SWEETER
THAN HONEY

One of the differences between an empty life and a full life is whether we've taken the opportunity to receive the truth of God in the deep places of our minds and hearts. God's truth is not merely information like the facts you comb the newspaper for. God's truth is a harvest in the heart. It is the life-changing comprehension of the reality of supernatural love. It is true knowledge of ourselves, true knowledge of God, and true knowledge of the world in which we live.

CONSUMING THE TRUTH

God longs for us to receive his word as contained in the Scriptures. To demonstrate this God had a prophet eat a scroll that tasted as sweet as honey in his mouth (Ezek. 3:3). Psalm 119:103 says, "How sweet are your words to my taste, sweeter than honey to my mouth."

To use another metaphor, think of the Bible as a topographical map of all reality. A hiker unfolds and studies a topographical map that describes with great detail the geography of where he stands—every hill, ravine, river, bridge, railroad, landmark, building. Then he knows how to proceed.

Scripture is God's top-down view, his published topographical map, of reality. Those who study it know of the gorges of evil, the mountaintops of God's holiness, the streams of fresh water, the roads leading to ruin, and the roads to good destinations. This knowledge is cumulative, of course, which is why we need to be devoted to a pattern of reading and studying Scripture. No one who is honest can say that he or she has a complete comprehension of truth, and those who do say that make us wary.

A yearning to hear God's voice will lead us to Scripture. If we read it naturally, widely, and over a long period of time, we will experience a filling that comes no other way. We will be assured and guided, and we will also be corrected and challenged (which is why Mark Twain said it wasn't the parts of the Bible he didn't understand that bothered him, but the parts he did understand).

FIRST HUNGER

One of the greatest joys I can think of are the times when I've been able to talk to people just as they have come to faith in Christ, smiles abounding just like in the delivery room of a hospital when a new life has noisily entered the world. Often people at that stage know they need to get their hands on a Bible, or the person who has led them to faith has given them a new, easy to understand Bible. The shrink-wrap is barely off it, the spine still cracks as they open it, and they have no idea where to find anything. You might as well say the Epistle to the Martians as the Epistle to the Romans, or the Gospel of Marx as the Gospel of Mark.

Then, six months later, they know where the Gospel of John is, and oh do they have questions! Six months after that, their Bible easily flops open on the desk, papers and notes spilling out, passages underlined and highlighted. But the truly impressive thing is the change in them. Holding a Bible that is getting more supple matters little; the miracle is the softening of the heart—and its strengthening and filling and expanding and deepening.

Who can explain such a supernatural process? It is an entirely different experience from being influenced by any other kind of book. A really good book with a great story or great ideas may get a grip on us and move us, but the discipline of assimilating Scripture into the mind and heart has a truly transforming effect.

WHY SCRIPTURE?

Here are God's own words about God's own Word:

Man does not live on bread alone but on every word that comes from the mouth of God.

—DEUTERONOMY 8:3; MATTHEW 4:4

How can a young person stay pure? By obeying your word and following its rules.... I have hidden your word in my heart, that I might not sin against you.... I weep with grief; encourage me by your word. Keep me from lying to myself; give me the privilege of knowing your law.... Your word is a lamp for my feet and a light for my path.

—PSALM 119:9, 11, 28–29, 105 NLT

The grass withers and the flowers fall, because the breath of the LORD blows on them. Surely the people are grass. The grass withers and the flowers fall, but the word of our God stands forever.

—ISAIAH 40:7–8

Let the word of Christ dwell in you richly as you teach and admonish one another with all wisdom.

—COLOSSIANS 3:16

For the word of God is living and active. Sharper than any double-edged sword, it penetrates even to dividing soul and spirit, joints and marrow; it judges the thoughts and attitudes of the heart.

—HEBREWS 4:12

All Scripture is God-breathed and is useful for teaching, rebuking, correcting and training in righteousness, so that the man of God may be thoroughly equipped for every good work.

—2 TIMOTHY 3:16

This last passage tells us that Scripture is "useful." Scripture is the spiritual breath of God that gives life, both by its immediate supernatural effect and by its practical usefulness in training. It teaches (tells us the truth), rebukes (confronts us when we violate the truth), corrects (shows us how to get back on track), and it trains in righteousness (disciplines us to stay on track).

BECOMING A LIFE LEARNER

How, then, do we make Scripture reading and study rich disciplines in our lives? Here are some fundamental guidelines.

1. Just read it. Don't wait until you have a master plan for consuming the whole of Scripture. Don't wait until things are just right or until you have a large block of time to read Scripture. Avoidance keeps us from God's voice, and simple procrastination does the same. When my grandfather was teaching me how to fish and watched me fiddling with my tackle, playing with bobbers and hooks and sinkers (with which I was utterly fascinated), he told me, "You won't catch any fish unless your line is in the water. Just fish!" And I found out that he was right. I never once caught a fish when my line was out of the water. It is guaranteed. I've thought of that lesson many times when I suspect I've been keen on talking about the theory of spiritual life instead of just doing it.

Just read it. Before you go to bed, read just one chapter or just a few verses. Commit to opening your Bible at least once every day. If you want to grow a garden, you've got to get the seed in the ground. Years ago my wife and I had a beautiful vegetable garden. I found that I really enjoyed tilling the ground in the spring (another personal fascination with equipment, I'm afraid), then enriching the soil with loam and natural fertilizer, and then tilling it many times over until the consistency was smooth and spongy—dirt that looked good enough to eat. But it is all pointless unless you get to the store, buy the seeds, and get them in the ground. You can cultivate, rake, and prepare the soil all you want, but with no seed in the ground, you haven't even begun.

Just read it.

2. Join your reading with praying. Again, if you are only beginning this discipline, don't worry about the form and the quantity. Pray

"Open my eyes that I may see wonderful things in your law" (Ps. 119:18). And after you've read, take a few minutes to quietly reflect on the thoughts prompted by the passage. Tell God what you've learned, what you want to thank him for, and ask for further guidance.

3. *Read and trust.* When we read Scripture, seeds *are* being planted. We may not see immediately how the story of Solomon, Paul's letter to Titus, or the book of Revelation will benefit us today. But as surely as seeds that are planted in rich, loamy soil with plenty of moisture will sprout, grow, and flourish, so will faithful daily readings of Scripture. Jesus taught about the Word of God in terms of seed that sometimes falls on the path (deaf ears), sometimes falls on rocky, shallow soil (superficial interest), and sometimes falls on soil choked with weeds (worldly competition). But when the seed falls into the heart of someone who is really listening and who trusts that God has spoken out of his love, then a living crop of truth will come to be. It just takes time and trust and a discipline that gets the seed planted in the first place.

John Wesley offered the following six suggestions for how we can develop a pattern of reading Scripture regularly, faithfully, thoughtfully, and effectively.

1. Set apart a little time every morning and evening.
2. Read one chapter out of the Old Testament and one chapter out of the New, or just read one chapter or a part of a chapter.
3. Read with "a single eye." In other words, read with a "fixed resolution" to know God's will as expressed in Scripture.
4. Constantly look for connections between what you are reading and what you've read elsewhere in Scripture. This is extremely important and gives us the joy of having the larger themes of Scripture come into clearer focus. Keep putting it together. Synthesize what you're reading with what you've read in the past. This method is called "the analogy of faith," because you are comparing what you are reading today with the truth of the whole faith. Solid conviction is born in our hearts as the notes sounded in Scripture flow together into harmonies that are repeated over and over.

5. Begin with prayer, because "Scripture can only be understood through the same Spirit whereby it was given," and end with prayer so that the Word will be written on your hearts.
6. Pause as you read. Reflect on how the passage applies to your life. Try to apply what you have read soon after you've read it.

To use Wesley's own words: "And whatever light you then receive should be used to the uttermost, and that immediately. Let there be no delay. Whatever you resolve begin to execute the first moment you can. So shall you find this word to be indeed the power of God unto present and eternal salvation."

FOR PERSONAL REFLECTION

1. When has a knowledge of Scripture been important in your life? When has it been "useful" for teaching, rebuking, correcting, or training in righteousness?

2. Has developing a habit of Scripture reading been easy or difficult for you? Explain why.

3. What are three or four topics in Christian belief that you would like to understand more fully in the years to come?

UNDERSTANDING SCRIPTURE

Let's say you've become convinced that the Bible just may have the truth and the power you know you need in your life, and you go out and purchase a brand-new Bible because you want to make a new beginning. You remove the wrapping and are pleased by the smell of new leather, holding it to your nose. Its pages are clean and white, the printing and binding done with far more care than any average book. This is the Word of God. Read more widely than any other book in history, it has been the foundation of whole systems of law; it has shaped whole civilizations. When translated, the Bible has become a defining landmark in culture and language, like the English version authorized during the reign of King James I of England or like the German version meticulously rendered by Martin Luther.

Most remarkably, the Bible has been a transforming power in the lives of millions of people, young and old, in every corner of the world, and across all the generations.

But how does the truth and power of God get from the printed page into your mind and heart?

READING WITH UNDERSTANDING

Reading Scripture with understanding is critical. Understanding begins by simply reading the words of Scripture. Whether the reading is done in a soft chair at home, in a hotel room, on a park bench, or in a meeting at a church, we are engaging in an inherently valuable pattern of devotion. But we need to seek understanding in what we read, not being discouraged or intimidated by those who believe that the Bible is open to anyone's arbitrary interpretation.

Here are a few basic principles of the interpretation of Scripture. If we follow these principles, we will get out of the Bible what God put into it, which is the only thing we should be interested in. If we want to read our own preconceived opinions into Scripture, we might as well be reading a novel, a biography, or a cookbook instead of the Bible.

Simple and Natural

The simplest and most natural understanding of a biblical passage is always the best. Because God chose to use human authors in writing the words of Scripture instead of dropping the Bible from the sky, we are supposed to read those words the way we would any other written communication. Paul wrote a letter to his friends in the city of Philippi, and they read it looking for the plain and simple meaning of what he intended to get across. If you get a letter from your mother, you open it, read it carefully and thoughtfully, and assume that she meant specific and concrete things by what she wrote. So it is with our reading of Jeremiah or Luke or Philippians. Ask yourself: what message was Jeremiah trying to get across to his listeners? What did Luke want people to get from his "orderly account"? What effect did Paul want his words about joy to have on his friends in Philippi?

Yes, of course there are statements in Scripture that are hard to understand, but we should focus on what is plain and clear and trust that sooner or later we will understand the more enigmatic sayings. Most of the Bible is straightforward when we take the time to read it carefully.

It Can Never Mean What It Never Meant

The Bible cannot mean what it never meant. We do not make the Bible meaningful; we discover its meaning. It is common for people to say, "This passage means such and such to me," but it would be far better for us to say, "It seems like John meant such and such, and here is how it applies to my life." If we import meaning into the Bible instead of exporting meaning, then we are using the Bible as a writing tablet for our own preconceived ideas and opinions. Better to use clean paper for that than paper that is already printed on. We are putting words into God's mouth and are then taking those words as authoritative. When friends do that to friends or kids do that to parents, we call it unfair and misleading. So it is with fanciful and arbitrary readings of Scripture. God has given us a body of truth that is wide enough and deep enough for a lifetime—no, for eternity! We don't need to add to Scripture. And if we try to add to it, we end up confusing its essence.

The Way Words Work

Appreciate the figurative language of Scripture for what it means. The Bible was written by dozens of authors over thousands of years in several different nations and in three different languages. Some of the Bible is history (like 1 and 2 Kings), some is poetry (the Psalms), some is symbolic story (the parables), some is law (Deuteronomy). The figurative expressions of Scripture have a special directness: "As the deer pants for streams of water, so my soul pants for you, O God." "I am the good shepherd." "Run the good race." Such phrases plant truths squarely and solidly in our minds.

We should never consider figurative language, whether metaphor, symbol, or parable or any other figurative language, a second-best way of communicating meaning. When we say that we read the Bible "literally" and only admit something is symbolic if we really need to, then we are showing how much the modern scientific worldview (in which measurable things are all that matter) has shaped us.

We use the word *literal* in two different ways, which unfortunately has caused some confusion. One day when my wife came in the house drenching wet and said, "It's literally raining cats and dogs out there," I couldn't help but say, "You mean, literally? Are they poodles or German shepherds or tabbies?" which of course drew a bemused look from her. What she meant was "It's *really* raining," which is technically not the meaning of *literally*. When someone says they believe the Bible is literally true, meaning "really true," I'd agree with them. I would disagree with someone, however, who says that they believe the only proper reading of Scripture is when every detail is to be taken literally. Jesus is not literally a door.

We should let the symbols and figures of Scripture sound aloud the theological truths they point to. The Hebrews and the Greeks knew the power of metaphor and symbol, and so they could read that God is a rock or a fortress or a shepherd or a light in the darkness and just let the power of the truth sink in. And, more to the point, God chose to use language in all its varied forms to give us a revelation that has literal detail *and* figurative power, history with poetry.

The Best Book on Bible Interpretation

Let Scripture interpret Scripture. This is extraordinarily important. When you read a passage and wonder what "resurrection" really means or "the kingdom of God" or "sexual immorality" or "Passover" or "antichrist" or "marriage," there is one place to turn: the rest of the Scriptures. Yes, archaeologists may have some relevant information, and there may be parallels in modern literature, science, or history, but Scripture is its own best interpreter. The New Testament passages about baptism are best explained by the other dozen or so passages about baptism and by the ritual of washing in the Old Testament, not by historical information about the use of water in the Egyptian cult of Isis. The Lord's Supper is best interpreted by all the other passages about this event, by Jesus' "I am the bread" teaching and by Old Testament descriptions of meals like Passover and the manna sent from heaven. Most of the incredible images and numbers from the book of Revelation, which puzzle people and which have produced wildly differing interpretations, have already appeared earlier in the Bible (for example, the mark on the forehead, a beast rising up out of the sea, and the numbers one thousand, seven, and twelve). Each image and number has a vivid meaning, and it is amazing how much easier it is to understand if we look up just one or two other passages that use the same language.

This analogy of faith is the comparison and synthesis of the various parts of the faith. Art is about repetition and variation, as are history and theology. God gives us a truth like "I am your Savior," and then he repeats it a hundred different ways throughout Scripture. Repetition and variation. Patterns. The words change slightly, metaphors are used, and through it all—by the words of the prophets and the apostles—God's word comes through strong and clear. We see the form of it all. Its lines become clearer and bolder. Conviction firms up in our minds and hearts.

This is why we must read Scripture as a rhythmic discipline of our lives. The Bible is a big book. It is full of epic stories, of oracles, sermons, prophecies, letters, songs, and proverbs and addresses the whole of life. It reveals God in all his actions and attributes. The Bible is a vivid mosaic of hundreds of personal stories in which people are trying to find God or trying to make or be their own god. It explains the issues of the twenty-first century as precisely as it does the issues of any other century. It is the best guide to life for people of all ages and backgrounds. It is the only direct and pure expression of God's own mind.

When we read Scripture as if studying a tapestry, we build a comprehensive structure of truth for our lives. We will see the patches of truth emerge and converge into a great patchwork. We'll be able to say, "Oh, so that's what joy means!" as we put together the pattern of what we read in Psalms and in Luke and in Philippians. We'll be able to say, "I now understand temptation because this passage in James explains what I read a while ago in Romans and in Matthew." Because certain themes come up so often, we'll be able to distinguish major themes that God wants us to understand (such as sanctification or forgiveness or sin) from minor themes that should not be our focus (such as where Jesus was between his death and resurrection).

Apply the Meaning

Apply the words of Scripture to life by carrying over the principles you discover in the original meaning of the biblical text. If I were to say that I should bring grace and truth into my relationships because in Jesus' parable the Samaritan soothed the wounds of the beaten-up man by applying oil and wine, I would be right—but for the wrong reason. Jesus sends no signal that oil and wine represent grace and truth, so I shouldn't apply the passage that way. When I read the parable of the good Samaritan, as with any other biblical text, my duty and my privilege is to say, "This means to me what it meant to them, and now I can spend a lifetime applying the principle of Jesus' teaching about what it means to be a neighbor."

The Intimacy of Listening to God

Think of understanding Scripture as understanding a person. The Bible is God's word about himself to us. It is the speech of a sovereign Lord and a loving Father, it is the word about Jesus the Word, and it is the breath of the Spirit. This principle is not about literary criticism; it is about an act of grace unfolding in our lives. When we read Scripture we can pray something like the following prayer.

PRAY THIS

Holy Spirit, you inspired the writers of Scripture. Now please illumine my mind so that I may grasp the width, length, height, and depth of your truth and life. Amen.

FOR PERSONAL REFLECTION

1. When have you heard someone making a questionable interpretation of the Bible? What caused you to question it?

2. Which of the six principles listed above is a new thought to you? Can you apply it to your own reading of Scripture at this time in your life?

3. When reading the Bible, how do you deal with sections that truly puzzle you?

4. What parts of the Bible have been easiest for you to understand? Where is a good place for someone unfamiliar with the Bible to begin reading?

MEDITATION
AND MUSCLE

I love being around people who have so deeply taken the Word of God into their lives that it has shaped the very way they think, their over-all attitude toward life, their reactions to minor and major events, even their temperament. This is the fruit that the Holy Spirit develops in us, the fruit of love, joy, peace, patience, kindness, goodness, gentleness, faithfulness, and self-control. These are the signs that the Word of God has truly gotten lodged in the deepest part of who we are—in the heart, where opinions are formed and motives are birthed, where emotions are sparked and decisions are set.

People who possess the fruit of the Spirit do not try to impress others by quoting Scripture all the time, and they do not feel obligated to slap a verse on every event of life. They so respect Scripture that they avoid twisting it to suit their purposes. They read the Bible because they long to know God and to have a God-filled life. The Bible is never a weapon in their hands, nor a mere tool. It is more than an encyclopedia of spiritual knowledge. It is the voice of God—sometimes a whisper, sometimes a shout, but always a revelation of God's own pure character. The Bible is thus the wisdom of

God, the power of God, the love of God, the light of God, the truth of God.

ONLY DWELLING WILL DO

But how does the Word of God get firmly planted in us?

Whenever I have run across Colossians 3:16, which says, "Let the word of Christ dwell in you richly," it has always challenged and enthused and comforted me. "Dwell in you richly." Of course that's what God wants! I'm not a computer hard drive whose purpose is to collect more and more data. I'm not a student hoping against hope to get all the answers right on the final exam. I'm a member of God's household, and I get to learn with my brothers and sisters the meaning of God's Word as given through the prophets and the apostles. I can ask God to make that Word take root and dwell deep in my heart, so deeply that it won't get blown away by the winds of today's concerns. Nobody can take it away. And God's Word will not lie dormant. Like well-planted seed, it will sprout and grow, and then put down roots and finally be ready for harvesting and digesting. We take God's Word in as seed, but it grows to become a nourishing feast.

SPIRITUAL MUSCLE TISSUE

The way I look at people who have had a pattern of reading Scripture over the years is that the Word they consume faithfully is transformed into the spiritual muscle tissue of their lives. The Word of God actually becomes part of who they are.

These people do not view Scripture as a collection of magical sayings that work wonders when voiced, but they consistently act out of the truth of Scripture. Their reactions to people around them are governed by grace because, so to speak, they have a graduate degree in grace (in learning and in experience). They react with truth because their consciences have been trained and shaped to stay within the bounds of honest, authentic reality. Their instincts, which are as fallen as anyone else's, have been retrained. They don't even wonder, "What is the biblical thing to do or say?" because biblical ethics and ethos have become essential to who they are. This is what is promised in the new covenant when God said, "I will put my law in their minds and write it on their hearts" (Jer. 31:33).

"Let the word of Christ dwell in you richly as you teach and admonish one another with all wisdom, and as you sing psalms, hymns and spiritual songs with gratitude in your hearts to God." This passage says there are a variety of ways the Word of Christ goes deeply enough to dwell in us. Teaching is paramount, so we need to keep searching like eagles for teachers, authors, and Bible study leaders who explain and apply the Word faithfully. "Admonishing one another with wisdom" suggests a flow of quality conversation among believers about what they are learning from God. Singing praise is another powerful way the Word of God is carried deeply into our hearts. Singing "with gratitude in [our] hearts to God" is a way that the crusty and hardened exterior of our lives can be cracked open so that spiritual seeds can be planted and begin to live and grow.

Colossians 3:16 points out the connection of different forms of worship. Why sing? So the Word will dwell richly. Why a variety of sounds (psalms, hymns, spiritual songs)? So the Word will knock on every door of our hearts that is the least bit cracked open. Why teach? So the Word will be clearly explained and powerfully applied. Worship is not the span between the start and the end of singing but is a great and varied advance of the Word on our souls. God uses as many fronts as he needs to make us stop and listen.

MORE THAN READING: MEDITATION

And then there is meditation—a way of reading Scripture so that it has a chance to take root. *Meditation* is a word the Bible uses to describe a way of holding and pondering God's truth so that it sinks in. It is wise, pensive concentration.

At the edge of the Promised Land, Joshua told the people they were going to need real spiritual muscle; wars lay ahead. Three times at the Jordan River Joshua said, "Be strong and courageous," and then he said, "Do not let this Book of the Law depart from your mouth; meditate on it day and night, so that you may be careful to do everything written in it. Then you will be prosperous and successful" (Josh. 1:8).

The Psalms speak about meditating on the Word of God and continuing that meditation through every pulse of life. Psalm 119 describes a committed discipline of taking the Word in.

I meditate on your precepts and consider your ways.

—VERSE 15

Though rulers sit together and slander me, your servant will meditate on your decrees.

—VERSE 23

Let me understand the teaching of your precepts; then I will meditate on your wonders.

—VERSE 27

I lift up my hands to your commands, which I love, and I meditate on your decrees.

—VERSE 48

May the arrogant be put to shame for wronging me without cause; but I will meditate on your precepts.

—VERSE 78

Oh, how I love your law! I meditate on it all day long.

—VERSE 97

I have more insight than all my teachers, for I meditate on your statutes.

—VERSE 99

My eyes stay open through the watches of the night, that I may meditate on your promises.

—VERSE 148

Okay, now, be honest. Did you just skim over those verses, or did you ponder them? If you're like me, you will occasionally find yourself reading *over* quotations of Scripture instead of reading *through* them. How hurried we can be!

That's what Christian meditation is all about—turning hurry into rumination. Slowing from a run into a walk. Tasting and digesting instead of devouring. Meditation is the only way to build spiritual muscle for the good times and the tough times.

FOR PERSONAL REFLECTION

1. Read Psalm 119 (it's long!) and note all the different things it says about the believer's relationship to the Word of God (which in Old Testament language is also referred to as the "law," "precepts," and so on).

2. What do you need to do in order to meditate on Scripture?

3. What stands in our way from taking the time to mediate on God's Word?

4. How have you seen spiritual muscle develop from a steady pattern of Scripture study?

PRAYER AND THE PRESENCE OF GOD

A brokenhearted young woman one day confided to a friend things that no one knew was happening behind the closed doors of her home.

"I go running to close the patio doors because I don't want the neighbors to hear the yelling. It could be any of us—me, my daughter, or my husband. He's been drinking regularly again. Not just on the weekends. He goes right for the bottle as soon as he gets home from work. Then I blow up. I know it doesn't do any good. I just lose it. And I lose it all the time, for any simple reason. My daughter's taken up smoking, and by the way she's withdrawing and slipping in her grades; I'm pretty sure she's doing some kind of drugs. I found filthy magazines in the garage in a box under the workbench. And I know I'm hiding too. I make sure I get to the mailbox before anyone else so that I can get the credit card bills. If anybody knew how often I've been going to the mall and how much I've spent—well, they'd think it's just sick. It just seems like we're all on some kind of wicked merry-go-round. But it's not merry. It's all vicious cycles. Things are going faster and faster. And I don't know how to stop it and get off."

WHICH MERRY-GO-ROUND AM I ON?

When you hear the word *habit*, does it conjure up a negative or a positive reaction in you? We are, by nature, habitual creatures. A habit is simply a recurrent pattern of behavior that is acquired through frequent repetition, a way of acting that becomes so ingrained that we do it almost unconsciously. Because habits are actions done over and over again, they have powerful, cumulative effects. We know, for instance, that the entire condition of our bodies and brains are affected when we practice good habits of eating, sleeping, and exercise; whereas bad habits like smoking and substance abuse have an accumulative devastating effect on the body.

One of the many compelling reasons for us to develop patterns of devotion in our lives is that "old habits die hard." Sheer willpower may produce temporary external changes in our lives, but the transformation of our hearts and the shaping of our minds require a deeper work of God. Prayer is a habit that opens us up for God's Spirit to do that work. Prayer is not like occasionally phoning a good friend to keep in contact; it is more like a ship unfurling its sail, which snaps open, catching the wind (or rather, is caught by the wind) and propelling the ship mightily in the direction of the will of the wind.

HABIT OVERCOMES HABIT

"Habit overcomes habit" is a proposition in the classic work *The Imitation of Christ,* which was written five hundred years ago. This idea says that the best way to change the ugly, self-destructive patterns of our lives is to seek to develop good habits that will not merely supplant the bad but will unleash the power of God in our lives.

Prayer may sometimes seem like a small thing, but perhaps none of us realizes just how powerful the habit of prayer can be.

When we pray—whether alone or in public, briefly or at length, spontaneously or according to a schedule—we are exposed to the flow of God's grace and the light of his truth. When prayer becomes a habit, foul patterns of self-centeredness and narrow-mindedness are gradually undermined.

DISCOURAGEMENT ABOUT PRAYER

Now before we go any further, let's admit how challenging it is to pray. I have met few believers who have not felt inadequate in their praying. I know I often feel that way. For many of us, discouragement comes simply from feeling that we have not prayed enough. And those who pray regularly and frequently are often disappointed about the depth or quality or content of their prayers.

Any of us can easily become paralyzed by the problems we face in prayer, and then the paralysis becomes the main problem.

But we can take comfort in this. God knows we're creatures of the earth. He certainly knows that the downward pull in our hearts, operating like a powerful gravitational force, often retards the desire to pray. The Bible tells us that we don't know what to pray for (Rom. 8:26). Jesus said to pray, "Our Father . . . ," so perhaps it shouldn't surprise us if we feel small and immature when we pray.

Question after question presses upon our minds and pushes us downward: Do I have time to pray? Won't God be insulted if I pray just a bit this morning? Are my scrambled words worthy of God? What if my attitude isn't right when I pray? What if I ask God for things he doesn't want to do? Why do my prayers always sound the same? Is it okay to use someone else's prayer as my own? What's the use of praying if God already knows what he intends to do?

Hesitation is the black hole into which a galaxy of unspoken prayers has been swallowed. The way to get past hesitation is just to open our mouths and speak up. Whatever, whenever, however.

ORDINARY PRAYER

Prayer is always an act of faith. It begins with faith, must be carried through in faith, and finished in faith. Every ordinary prayer prayed in the most ordinary way by the most ordinary person is a revolutionary statement of trust. In prayer, we take a stand and say, "I have questions only God can answer, I have a longing only he can fill, I bear pain that only a crucified Lord can understand. I need to speak with God!"

When you read what the Bible says about prayer, it appears that God is far more interested in our bringing before him a steady flow of ordinary, even homely, prayers rather than great eruptions of spiritual energy. Prayer shapes us best as habit, a steady pulse of unhurried conversations with God. We have to trust that it is the right thing to do. And then we need to do it.

To establish prayer as habit, each of us needs to understand where and how we best pray. Some people pray best when they use the words of the Psalms or another prayer book. Some people find the quiet of early morning the time when they can best talk to God.

I'm not sure I know why, but I find it easiest to pray when I'm walking. Maybe sitting still allows too many distractions to fly around in my head. Maybe I concentrate best on my "walk" in life when I'm physically walking. Any walkway will do—a concrete sidewalk or an asphalt road; a footpath is even better. When I get a chance to walk in the woods, that's better still, but the best is walking along a shore. (And if a shore isn't available, just thinking about it does the trick.)

I was born in Chicago and since then I've lived four different phases of my life in different towns or cities on the western side of Lake Michigan, and I'm so grateful for that. Whenever I walk along the shore of that vast lake, it seems like walking along the edge of eternity. The landward side is the world of firm ground I belong to, but out across the water is another world that is alien to me, even threatening, with its depths and its waves and its brisk winds. Yet those two worlds are not opposed to each other. Our bodies are, after all, more than 70 percent water.

I think I like to walk along the shore of a lake or an ocean because it reminds me that we all walk on an edge between this world and eternity. When we pray we are acting as earth creatures casting our voices out to the expanse where God dwells. He is immanent and dwells in this world, to be sure, but because he is also beyond this world, our connections with him (often made concrete in prayer) save us in this world.

Patterns of devotion are not our brilliant ideas of how we can reach God. They are God's loving invitations to interact with him.

The Bible invites us to trust and then to speak up rather than be closed up.

Here are just some of those invitations:

- "Be joyful in hope, patient in affliction, faithful in prayer" (Rom. 12:12).
- "Devote yourselves to prayer, being watchful and thankful" (Col. 4:2).
- "They devoted themselves . . . to prayer" (Acts 2:42).
- "Then Jesus told his disciples a parable to show them that they should always pray and not give up" (Luke 18:1).
- "And pray in the Spirit on all occasions with all kinds of prayers and requests. With this in mind, be alert and always keep on praying for all the saints" (Eph. 6:18).
- "The end of all things is near. Therefore be clear minded and self-controlled so that you can pray" (1 Peter 4:7).
- "But you, dear friends, build yourselves up in your most holy faith and pray in the Holy Spirit" (Jude 20).

PRAYING ALL DAY

Many believers say they pray best when prayer is a continual dialogue with God through the course of the day. As one person put it, "I do not often pray for fifteen minutes straight, but hardly ever do fifteen minutes pass without my praying." This is obviously not the kind of prayer where someone is down on his knees in a quiet room of his house. Rather, it is the idea that one can say a sentence or two to God anytime, anywhere, out loud or silently. Done many times over during the course of a day, one develops a steady openness to God. Continual prayer allows one to respond to God at the moment one sees any special act or blessing from God. It is to ask God questions during the day, the whole day, about what you're seeing, the decisions you're making, your choice of words before they come out of your mouth.

A day spent in continual dialogue with God might go something like this:

- As you wake and that first rush of thoughts comes into your head about what you'll be doing that day, say to God, "Thank you for the chance to rest and to start again. Please help me to see you in this day and to please you by who I am today."
- You shower and as you relax all kinds of thoughts pop into your head. Some worries, some regrets, some ideas. Tell God, "I trust you, God. Teach me how to leave these concerns in your hands. Help me know what I should do."
- You take fifteen or twenty minutes in a quiet part of the house to read a chapter or two in the Bible. You begin by first saying to God, "Your Word is a lamp to my feet and a light for my path." When you've finished your reading, take a few quiet moments to meditate on what you've read and then talk to God about your response, thanking him for a truth you found, telling him what you don't understand, confessing where you sense you are coming up short.
- As you make your morning drive, thoughts of your work start emerging in your mind. Tell God, "This meeting concerns me. Help me figure out what is going on here. Help me to believe in your presence throughout this day."
- You're in a tense and tricky phone conversation. You have to decide what to say and when to hold your tongue. You pray silently, "Lord, give me the right words."
- You choose to have a light and brief lunch so that you have time to take a good walk. You get some fresh air, which gives you a chance to clear your head, and every so often you say something aloud or silently to God. You respond to the thoughts he brings to you with whatever is appropriate: thanks, praise, confession, or petition.
- During the afternoon, you again cast silent or verbal sentences to God during many situations. In one sense, it is like having your best friend next to you and discussing the unfolding of the day in a natural and engaging way. In another sense, however, you keep in the front of your mind that this is the Lord of heaven and earth you are talking to, and you welcome the sense of reverential awe that remembrance brings.

- A quiet moment before supper is a good moment for heartfelt thanks.
- Before you nod off to sleep, you say, "Dear God, help me to learn from what I experienced today. Thanks for the opportunity to live this day before you. Here is what I regret . . . Here is what I'm glad about . . . Please recharge me with rest."

PRACTICING THE PRESENCE OF GOD

Your days and your lifestyle may be very different from this example. But the same principles apply whether you are a student, or spend most of your day at home, or work in a factory.

Many Christians describe this way of praying as "the practice of the presence of God." Three hundred years ago a man who was a cook and a cleaner wrote an inspiring diary, in which he explained that his greatest passion in life was to grow spiritually to the point that he would be in a constant state of awareness of God's good presence. Nicholas Herman, or Brother Lawrence as he was later called, worked in a Parisian monastery. He called himself "a servant of the servants of God." Seeking a continual sense of the presence of God, he prayed and worshiped as he cooked and as he cleaned.

Brother Lawrence described his method of prayer as follows: "I have since given up all forms of devotions and set prayers except those which are suitable to this practice. I make it my business only to persevere in his holy presence wherein I keep myself by a simple attention and a general fond regard to God, which I refer to as an actual presence of God. Or, to put it another way, an habitual, silent, and secret conversation of the soul with God."

He worried that some would think his method suspicious: "I know that some will accuse me of inactivity, of delusion, and of self-love. I confess that it is a holy inactivity, and would be a happy self-love if the soul in that state were capable of it."

And he was probably right. Christians are absolutely notorious for being judgmental about the devotional practices of other Christians that seem a little different from what they are used to. What must God think of us for scrutinizing the most intimate part of each other's lives and for having the audacity to reject each other on such grounds.

This much surely any Christian will embrace: there can be nothing better than for us to be so God-conscious, so God-centered, that our thoughts, words, and deeds flow throughout ordinary days as a response to him. Does our own fallenness stand in the way of this? Certainly. Should we guard ourselves against spiritual triumphalism? Yes. But despite these things, we should never hold back from the desire to have as close of a daily communion with God as we can.

PRAY THIS

Both of these prayers focus on the idea of "Father, into your hands I commit my spirit," which were Jesus' last words on the cross, but which were also the words of a common Jewish daily prayer, almost like the modern "Now I lay me down to sleep."

A Morning Prayer

Dear Lord, as this day begins I confess that I will need you every moment. I long to know you more deeply today. Help me, Jesus, in what I say to other people. Give me wisdom in each decision I will make. Make love and truth the motives behind everything I do. And when I fall short, help me not to give up but to find an extra measure of your strength. This day is your creation and your gift. I commit my body and spirit to your good purposes. In Jesus' name, Amen.

An Evening Prayer

Dear Lord, as this day ends I am glad to be able to rest in you. I believe that you are with me and that you hear my prayer. May the good things that happened today be planted deeply in the memory of my heart and shape me into a better person. Help me to learn from my mistakes and my sins. Thank you for the promise of a new beginning tomorrow. Now allow me to rest body, mind, heart, and soul in you and you alone and to awake refreshed in the goodness of your care. In Jesus' name, Amen.

FOR PERSONAL REFLECTION

1. When has prayer come easily for you, and when has it been difficult?

2. What are the conditions most conducive to prayer for you? Why do these conditions help you to pray?

3. What do you think of the proposition "Habit overcomes habit"?

4. Study and meditate on the biblical passages cited in this chapter. How do they apply at this time in your life?

PRAY LIKE THIS

Waiting, again waiting. How much time they had spent waiting for him! Once again Jesus took his time in the solitude of prayer. While the disciples waited they had opportunity to think about things. They thought about the dramas unfolding before them. Withered hands healed, lame people walking, a dead girl now alive and playing in the streets again. Enemies hovering like vultures, crowds pressing in so many times. Things were often raised to a feverish pitch. So what was Jesus doing? He was off praying again. He didn't show off in public places like the priests in their prayers. He didn't care if he wasn't in a synagogue. All he needed was time alone. What was this all about? What is this kind of praying?

"One day Jesus was praying in a certain place. When he finished, one of his disciples said to him, 'Lord, teach us to pray, just as John taught his disciples.' He said to them, 'When you pray, say . . .'" (Luke 11:1–2).

WHY PRAY?

Why in the world does God want us to pray? Does God get something he wouldn't otherwise have if we pray to him? Is God waiting for instructions from us so he'll know what to involve himself in next? Is he looking for devotees who please him by cycling through a vocal ritual?

No, it appears as though God wants us to speak with him, and in turn to listen to him, so that we can grow in a living, dynamic relationship with him. Along the way we gain perspective, confidence, wisdom, and strength. Sometimes prayer isn't our strongest moment; sometimes prayer is a cry, but we are better off to have cried out to God than to have cried alone.

HOW SHOULD WE PRAY?

But how should we pray? In a teaching as clear and fresh as the blue Sea of Galilee, Jesus said, "This, then, is how you should pray,"

> Our Father in heaven,
> hallowed be your name,
> your kingdom come,
> your will be done
> on earth as it is in heaven.
> Give us today our daily bread.
> Forgive us our debts,
> as we also have forgiven our debtors.
> And lead us not into temptation,
> but deliver us from the evil one.
> —MATTHEW 6:9–13

This prayer is a clear, straightforward pattern for developing a God-filled life. Jesus did not say, "Pray this." He said, "This is *how* you should pray." In other words: Here is the model, a plan. If you follow this, you will have prayed well. Your attitude will be right, you will have asked for the right things, and you will be changed in the praying.

Sometimes we should simply pray the exact words of the Lord's Prayer. It is neither childish nor ritualistic to do so. We may have learned the alphabet and simple arithmetic when we were small children, but these fundamentals are not thereby a weaker reality; they are the core of linguistic and mathematic reality. So it is with the pattern called the Lord's Prayer.

The best thing we can do is to cherish the actual words of the Lord's Prayer but also let its ideas form our basic instincts as we approach God. One by one, each petition of the Lord's Prayer tells us how and what to pray.

Our Father in heaven

Whenever we pray we should address God in personal terms. We've been invited to speak to the Father, to the Lord Jesus, and to the Holy Spirit—and so we should do so. Prayers that address a vague, unknown deity are artificial and uncertain. We've got God's own permission to talk to him as Abba—our loving Father.

Hallowed be your name

Respect for God is the doorway to genuine prayer. An attitude that is flippant or disingenuous makes praying useless or even destructive. Jesus warned against the "babbling" of pagans who think they will be heard for their many words. He also had stern words for those who wanted to show off in front of others with their prayers, calling them "hypocrites." God doesn't ask us to impress him but to honor him. So when we pray, we should tell God in as many ways as come to mind what we appreciate about him.

Your kingdom come, your will be done on earth as it is in heaven

We sometimes add to our prayers phrases like "If it be your will" as a polite disclaimer or as an expression of agnosticism. But Jesus' prayer suggests that we should start by expressing our desire to know God's will. "Your kingdom come, your will be done" is our way of saying, "Lord, I really need to understand your heart and mind. Let my own heart and mind, like soft metal impressed by a die, understand and imitate what you call right and good."

Give us today our daily bread

God invites us to pray to him about the basic provisions of life. Even when there is little doubt in our minds that there will be food on the table, it is good to ask the Father for life and health so that when we have these things our eyes are open to the flow of God's common grace and we live in a consistent state of gratitude.

Forgive us our debts, as we also have forgiven our debtors

God does not forgive us because we ask him for forgiveness but because of his sacrificial love turned to action in Christ. But it is still good to ask for forgiveness—and to ask every day—because it makes us realize that we are flawed creatures in constant need of repair. The phrase "as we also have forgiven our debtors" is a great challenge. By inviting us to pray this way, Jesus was telling us not to ask to receive what we are unwilling to give. We will only comprehend the forgiveness of God if we embrace forgiveness by granting it to others.

And lead us not into temptation

By telling us to pray that God would protect us as we go through the strongest forms of temptation, Jesus is saying that it is crucial for us to be vigilant about the many possibilities of failure we face. We can't really ask God to isolate us from all temptation; the Bible tells us that we will be tempted. But we can and must ask God to protect us from the terrible temptation-failure combination. Martin Luther said, "You may not be able to prevent the birds from flying over your head, but you can prevent them from making nests in your hair."

But deliver us from the evil one

We can and should pray, every day in our own way, "Father, I know that evil is real. I know there are malevolent forces that seek to bring about injury, deception, and perversion. I know you are infinitely stronger than those forces. Please help me to continually trust in your absolute protection."

○ ○ ○

This, then, was the prayer form Jesus set out for us. Every word is gold. It says exactly what any person of any age living anywhere in the world at any time needs to pray. Each petition can be prayed a thousand different ways. Each can be customized to the specifics of our lives.

PRAY THIS

This prayer is a spectacular prayer of the apostle Paul (Eph. 3:14–19 NLT) emphasizing the fullness that Christ brings. Pray these things for yourself or for someone else.

> *When I think of the wisdom and scope of God's plan, I fall to my knees and pray to the Father, the Creator of everything in heaven and on earth. I pray that from his glorious, unlimited resources he will give you mighty inner strength through his Holy Spirit. And I pray that Christ will be more and more at home in your hearts as you trust in him. May your roots go down deep into the soil of God's marvelous love. And may you have the power to understand, as all God's people should, how wide, how long, how high, and how deep his love really is. May you experience the love of Christ, though it is so great you will never fully understand it. Then you will be filled with the fullness of life and power that comes from God.*

PRACTICE THIS

Find a quiet half hour or more sometime this week and write out your own paraphrase of the Lord's Prayer. Write the same ideas as in each petition but as they apply to your life right now. Use this prayer during the week.

If you haven't recently prayed the exact words Jesus used, then do that, using quiet meditation following each petition to ask God to apply its meaning to your life.

FOR PERSONAL REFLECTION

1. Do you remember a pivotal time when you heard the Lord's Prayer used or when you used it yourself? If so, why did this prayer have impact at that time?

2. Putting yourself in the place of Jesus' listeners on that plain beside the Sea of Galilee, what would have been going through your mind as you heard Jesus laying out this teaching on prayer?

3. What do you make of Jesus' critique of those who pray by "babbling" many words and those who pray for public show (Matt. 6:5–8)?

4. How do you think the ideas in the Lord's Prayer can be helpful to you at this time in your life? Which petitions are especially important for you?

COME TO
THE MOUNTAIN

Yesterday I finished some meetings in Colorado and had the better part of the day to drive into the heart of the spectacular Rocky Mountains. My small rental vehicle just happened to have four-wheel drive, so I couldn't resist an off-road path that led straight up a mountain near the timberline at 12,000 feet, where perfect arrow-shaped pine trees get sparser and sparser and you can see pockets of snow and ice even now, in August. But the thin air, the piercing sun, the rocks and deep ruts of the path, and a threatening thunderstorm that sent booming blasts across the rock combined to make me feel like I was in someone else's world, and I resigned and headed back down.

A mile lower in altitude, I was surrounded by mountains on all sides—an entirely different feeling, which alternately seemed ominous and comforting. I took a walk in this beautiful place, hoping to pray seriously, but was absorbed with the many thoughts bouncing around in my head. So, frustrated and embarrassed, I just focused on the Lord's Prayer, letting each phrase dictate to my mind what I should be thinking and praying.

In a way I'm glad I didn't grow up around mountains, because when I occasionally get to visit them, they always leave me in awe. And they always help me spiritually. I would not want to ever take the mountains for granted.

COMING TO THE MOUNTAIN

At several key turning points in his life, Jesus went to a mountain to pray. Why is that? We know that it parallels Moses' encounters with God on Mount Sinai. We know that as Moses was transformed by meeting with God so that his face was radiant, Jesus was transfigured on a mountain, with Peter, James, and John as witnesses. In Scripture mountains are always the symbol of permanence and might. They are, to us lowlanders, a kind of intersection between heaven and earth. So God beckons us to come to the mountain.

What Mount Sinai was for Moses and the slaves freed from Egypt and what the mount of transfiguration was for Peter, James, and John, prayer is for us. Prayer is about meeting with God. It is not a sanctified place, but a sanctified moment. Like the mountains, prayer is a meeting where we are to be awed, alarmed, comforted, and consoled all at the same time. Unlike coming to the mountains, however, we now come to the good and gracious Lord Jesus, as it says in Hebrews 12:

> You have not come to a mountain that can be touched and that is burning with fire; to darkness, gloom and storm; to a trumpet blast or to such a voice speaking words that those who heard it begged that no further word be spoken to them, because they could not bear what was commanded.... But you have come to Mount Zion, to the heavenly Jerusalem, the city of the living God. You have come to thousands upon thousands of angels in joyful assembly, to the church of the firstborn, whose names are written in heaven. You have come to God, the judge of all men, to the spirits of righteous men made perfect, to Jesus the mediator of a new covenant, and to the sprinkled blood that speaks a better word than the blood of Abel.
> —VERSES 18–20, 22–24

We must hold in our minds and hearts this meaning of prayer, no matter how much our hurried and hassled lives cause us to pray as if we are shouting quick instructions to the kids upstairs or cause us not to pray at all.

How can we set a habit of prayer that will be true to the meaning of prayer?

A SIMPLE WAY TO PRAY

Clip, clip. Snip, snip. Clumps of thick Saxon hair fell around the man's shoulders and dropped to the floor. The barber, one Peter Beskendorf, engaged his customer in one more conversation about spiritual matters. "Pastor," he said, "how should I pray? How long should I go on? What exactly should I say?"

We don't know what the man in the chair—Dr. Martin Luther of Wittenberg—said, but we do know that Peter Beskendorf's questions prompted Luther to write a small book called *A Simple Way to Pray*.

Here is an excerpt from this heartfelt bit of pastoral advice on prayer:

> Dear Master Peter: I will tell you as best I can what I do personally when I pray. May our dear Lord grant to you and to everybody to do it better than I! Amen.
>
> When I feel that I have become cool and joyless in prayer because of other tasks or thoughts (for the flesh and the Devil always impede and obstruct prayer), I take my little Psalter, hurry to my room, or, if it be the day and hour for it, to the church where a congregation is assembled and, as time permits, I say quietly to myself and word-for-word the Ten Commandments, the Creed, and, if I have some time, some words of Christ or of Paul, or some psalms, just as a child might do.
>
> It is a good thing to let prayer be the first business of the morning and the last at night. Guard yourself carefully against those false, deluding ideas which tell you, "Wait a little while. I will pray in an hour; first I must attend to this or that." Such thoughts get you away from prayer into other affairs which so hold your attention and involve you that nothing comes of prayer for that day.

It may well be that you may have some tasks which are as good or better than prayer, especially in an emergency. . . . When your heart has been warmed by such recitation to yourself (of the Ten Commandments, the words of Christ, etc.) and is intent upon the matter, kneel or stand with your hands folded and your eyes towards heaven and speak or think as briefly as you can, "O Heavenly Father, dear God, I am a poor unworthy sinner. I do not deserve to raise my eyes or hands toward you or to pray. But because you have commanded us all to pray and have promised to hear us and through your dear Son Jesus Christ have taught us both how and what to pray, I come to you in obedience to your word, trusting in your gracious promise."

Luther then suggests praying the Lord's Prayer, word for word, elaborating on things that come to mind. He then continues:

Take care, however, not to undertake all of this or so much that one becomes weary in spirit. Likewise, a good prayer should not be lengthy or drawn out, but frequent and ardent. . . . With practice one can take the Ten Commandments on one day, a psalm or chapter of Holy Scripture the next day, and use them as flint and steel to kindle a flame in the heart.

BEYOND UNDERSTANDING

That inquisitive barber knew, like the apostle Paul did, that prayer begins with the confession that "we do not know what we ought to pray for" and then discovering day by day that "the Spirit helps us in our weakness" (Rom. 8:26).

As a pastor, one of the luxurious blessings I receive is the sincere and intent prayers of people in our church. Often people will tell me, with a clear-eyed look of complete sincerity, that they pray for me and my family regularly. I always immediately feel like a huge gift has been given me tied up in large gold bows. It is something I don't take for granted. I know that in ways too mysterious for us to understand, such prayers bear us along.

And in the end, I don't think I need to understand how this works. It is probably good for me that there is a great mystery to it all. That way I can just keep praying, just talking to God, and being built in faith.

REHEARSING THE GREAT TRUTHS

One of the most amazing things about prayer, I think, is how the moment a prayer begins, even before the first breath vibrates our vocal chords, we are acting on several great truths only grasped by faith.

We are under God (prayer as position). Prayer is fundamentally an act of submission. Whenever we pray with the proper respect for God's position and character, we are rehearsing our place in the grand scheme of things. Nothing is better for the soul than that.

We are with God (prayer as presence). Why speak to the open air unless you think someone is listening? If we believe God hears us, then he must be with us.

We are in God (prayer as power). The moment we begin to pray we are reinforcing the conviction that God is acting all around us. His kingdom has come. We stand in the midst of his mighty deeds. So prayer must have immense power—not its own power, but the power of God.

We are for God (prayer as purpose). Prayer is the contemplative leading edge of mission. The moment we begin praying for God to bless the endeavors we make in his name, we are strengthening our understanding that we are in this world on a great mission for God. This is not a world of lieutenants, sergeants, and colonels; every soldier has the same equipment.

PRAY THIS

O Son of God, perform a miracle for me; change my heart. You, whose crimson blood redeems mankind, whiten my heart. It is you who makes the sun bright and the ice sparkle; you who makes the rivers flow and the salmon leap. Your skilled hand makes the nut tree blossom and the corn turn golden; your spirit composes the songs of the birds and the buzz of the bees. Your creation is a million wondrous miracles, beautiful to behold. I ask of you just one more miracle: beautify my soul.

—CELTIC PRAYER

FOR PERSONAL REFLECTION

1. How do you think Luther's advice to his barber might apply in your life?
2. What good experiences with prayer can you hold on to and preserve the future?
3. Why do you think the apostle Paul said that we do not know what we should pray? How is it that God's Spirit helps us know what to pray?

THAT ROOM

Imagine you walk into a large empty room with just the clothes on your back. But you carry a whole world with you: your joys and sorrows, doubts and confidence, beliefs and misconceptions, selfishness and altruism, hope and discouragement, stress and strength. It is just you and the world you carry with you that no one else but God can really see and understand.

When you walk out of that room a while later, your burdens seem a bit lighter and you don't feel so alone. Your mind is churning through a new way of looking at your life, and your spirit seems softer because it has been opened up and loosened. There are other people around you who smile, and a few who recognize you extend their hands to shake yours. You cannot put it into words, but you have a sense that something very right has just happened. You've been through a dignifying passage, a holy encounter. You realize that you are connected not just with this world you live in but with another mysterious world where a different set of rules apply and powerful and meaningful things happen more often than we can imagine. And you realize that this "kingdom of God" is not contained in the room you just left; you are walking in it. You remain in it when you go to work and when you sit down at the dinner table. But that room helped you realize it more fully. And you wonder when you can go back to that wonderful room again and what will happen to you if you keep going back.

IT'S NOT REALLY ABOUT THE ROOM

The room I am talking about is that place in our lives called worship. Sometimes worship happens in actual rooms, and how different these rooms can look! The worship room may be a four-hundred-year-old stone chapel with stained glass, or a high-tech auditorium with video screens and racks of lights, or a refugee shelter with a tin roof and walls made of plastic tarps supplied by the UN. The early Christians used the underground crypts known as the catacombs, where they could have privacy. Nobody else would think of having meetings in burial chambers. For persecuted Christians today, a barn, a cellar, or someone's living room will do—as long as the singing is kept to a hush.

It is, of course, not about the room at all. God is on the loose. He is not limited to a temple, nor is he limited to the latest greatest trend in worship style. We may think of ourselves as seeking God when we gather for worship, but the first question between the human race and God was not man saying, "Where are you, God?" but God saying to the man hiding in the trees of the garden, "Where are you?" (Gen. 3:9).

TRUE WORSHIP

Before we ever thought to seek God, he was seeking us. And he is still seeking. Jesus said the Father is seeking a certain kind of worshiper, people who will worship "in spirit and truth" (John 4:23). The Samaritan woman Jesus was speaking to tried to tell Jesus it was about the room ("You Jews worship in Jerusalem, but we worship on Mount Gerizim"). No, Jesus said it is not the room that is important but spirit and truth. Those are the qualities that make true worship, and true worshipers.

In worship the Spirit of God does a work on the spirit of a person; the Spirit of Truth puts a deeper truth into the mind of the worshiper. And when that is done time and again, year after year, in good times and in bad—when worship is an intentional and consistent pattern of life—we are profoundly shaped. Worship is a nonnegotiable; we must worship.

That's a hard sell for people who think only of unpleasant experiences when they think of worship. Why is it so easy for us to talk about unsatisfactory experiences in public worship? One reason is that there are a thousand ways we fickle creatures just mess it up. When pastors teach nonsense or fill the air with empty words, when musicians use worship as their stage, when we impress ourselves with our own splendor, we have failed before we even begin.

Sometimes we feel disappointed about worship, however, not because the public worship is corrupt but because as worshipers we have focused on the wrong things. Anyone can scrutinize and grouse about the details of worship. But if we make God our focus by coming into "that room" with an attitude of hope and expectancy and a resolve that we will pray to the living God, we will praise him, we will listen to his living Word, then something good is going to happen.

BOWING AND SERVING: THE WHOLE MEANING OF WORSHIP

The Bible shows us the proper focus by telling us two important purposes of worship. The first is bowing or bending the knee; the other is service.

When Jesus' disciples "worshiped" him in the boat after he had calmed the stormy Sea of Galilee, when Mary "worshiped" Jesus in the garden of resurrection, and when the Magi from the east brought gifts and "worshiped" Jesus, what happened is that they all bowed low before Jesus. To bow or to bend the knee is a way of saying to God, "I am here before you to submit to your greatness. You are all-wise and all-powerful, ever-present and ever-active. I am alive because of you, and I'll know how to live only if I get instructions from you. I need you as Teacher, Physician, Shepherd, Fortress,

Father, Counselor, Friend. I worship you because no one and nothing else is worthy of worship."

Worship is service in that it is something we do for God first and foremost, and if we are blessed in return (which we always will be), then wonderful! But we must begin by believing and by saying, "I do things for myself all week long, God. I ask for your help in every circumstance of my life. Now I am here, with these other people, and I wish to serve you. I will sing words of praise because you are the greatest Great and highest Good. I delight in serving you. I want to be used by you."

Now, there is much to be said about the practice of worship, and we'll come to that later, but there is nothing more important than for us to stay focused on these two purposes of worship.

When we come to "that room" with a single-hearted intent to bow and to serve, we will carry from that room, into all of the rooms of our lives, the same dynamic interaction with God. Our lives aren't filled by God when we just come to a God-filled sanctuary once a week but when that God-filled time of public worship is the rehearsal for a whole week of bowing and serving. That is the reason we engage in both public worship (with a community of other worshipers) and personal worship (when we direct all our acts of submission and service in adoration of God).

ENTERING THAT ROOM

Here are some things we can do in that room that will help us be "true worshipers."

- Focus on what makes you think about God. If you are distracted by the clothing of a singer or the tuning of a guitar or the gestures of the preacher, then ask God to help your mind focus on more important things.
- Sing with your heart. Don't be discouraged if you can't hold a tune, and don't impress yourself by how good you sound.
- Listen carefully when the words of Scripture are read. Hang on every word; let each one sink in. Believe that these seeds will sprout at some point.

- Decide to take away one new insight from the teaching, and hold on to it.
- When you are being led in prayer, pray yourself. Don't think of it as a time to listen to someone else praying but as an opportunity for you to ride on the choice phrases of the prayer.
- Trust in the purposes of worship. Even if you don't feel like bowing or serving, or if in the last month you haven't felt that worship has had any positive affect on you, believe that it is still inherently right to be obedient to God in this way.
- Let worship leaders and planners know when you were especially blessed in worship. They want to know what is happening in the congregation, so tell them.
- As you leave worship, avoid talking about the service like a movie critic evaluating a show. Don't focus on what you didn't care for. Tell someone else about an insight you gained or an encouragement you received.

FOR PERSONAL REFLECTION

1. Describe an experience of worship or a period of time in your life when worship had a significant impact on your life.
2. What stands in the way between you and God in the act of worship?
3. What special meaning do the ideas of bowing before God and serving him have for you at this time in your life?

FILLING
THE CHASM

On Sunday morning, September 16, 2001, people crowded our church like we usually see only on a holiday like Christmas or Easter. This non-holiday, precipitated by the unholy events of September 11, was a scurrying to God. The mood was unlike anything I've ever experienced. People were subdued and sober. They spoke sparingly to each other. People came with a kind of chasm in their hearts. We could all sense it. Not only were hearts blasted open, but we could sense what was really inside, where there was strength and where there was weakness.

THE TRIED AND TRUE PRACTICES OF WORSHIP

If ever there was a time to worship, this was it. And the time-honored, tried-and-true practices of worship were exactly the pattern we all needed: singing of praise, reading of Scripture and teaching of its meaning, prayer, offering, the Lord's Supper.

One of the most important lessons I will take away from those days is the longing that we have for the voice of God. The power of the words of Scripture—the ring of its truth and the energy of its life—asserted itself on us. In all the special prayer meetings and worship services whenever the voice of God in Scripture was sounded, we listened like people whose attention is arrested by a trumpet.

We read many Psalms in those days. I heard from numerous people that they instinctually turned to those treasured pages in the center of the Bible. Why was that? Was it because many of the Psalms are prayers voiced by people like David whose hearts were torn wide open, their treasures and their chasms revealed? Was it because the Psalms cry out to God in a plea for moral certitude and for the assurance that God is with us? Probably that and much more. God's voice gives us a voice when reality exceeds our ability to form words.

People did want to raise their own voices in praise. The singing of praise came from somewhere deep within. People used worship as their opportunity to shout out their convictions about truth and righteousness and the holy love of God. Far better than writing a letter to the editor of the local newspaper, worship was and is an opportunity to publish what you believe, to assert it solidly for others to hear, for God to hear, and for yourself to hear. There is true praise and there is false praise ("Those who forsake the law praise the wicked," Prov. 28:4), so the action of adoration is an act of moral and spiritual discernment. Praise is a way of tracing and retracing the lines of moral definition. It establishes in our minds and hearts the specific forms of spiritual character.

As that week unfolded, our plan for Sunday's worship service changed by the day. What might God want to do with this worship service? How can the people that will gather go away knowing unequivocally that God is with us?

We were so glad that communion was going to be part of that worship service. What better way to review the truth that God is with us than to take the bread and take the cup that are Christ's assertion that he intends to dwell in our lives, that he will go with us into every circumstance, that his presence is a pure gift to us. We had pastors and elders and their wives positioned throughout the sanctuary so that people could get up out of their seats to come and receive the bread and the cup from the leaders who loved them and wanted to support them. It was a moment I will never forget.

Worship on September 16, 2001, was unlike any other time, yet it was like every other time. Worship, like all devotion, is powerfully influential in our lives if it is a continual rhythm of life. We have to come back week after week. I grieved knowing that the hundreds of extra people in church on September 16 probably wouldn't come back the following weeks despite warm invitations—which is exactly what happened.

So what are we to learn from all this?

WORSHIP WORKS

Worship "works" (if you can put it that way) when it happens regularly, week after week, opening an ever-wider conversation with God. It took massive explosions and the instant perishing of thousands to open the hearts of some people to God. Shopping malls were closed, but churches were open (the first time we can remember that happening!). Where else can you go with a chasm in your heart but to God?

A time of crisis is a call to preparedness. Government agencies, transportation companies, and private citizens respond by intense self-examination: What could we have done? What should we have done? What must we do now?

The spiritual lesson of the hour is that we *must* worship. In worship we gain a pattern of truth that enables us to comprehend the ebb and flow of good and evil in the world; we establish an open line of communication with God so that we know how to find his mercy at any time in our lives. In worship we gain a vision of God, who is more solid than the mountains. Worship establishes the meaning of our citizenship in the kingdom of God so that we can be better citizens in our own society. Worship binds us to each other in a family that cannot be nullified.

No matter the differences of style of public worship, the core practices themselves are remarkably constant no matter where you go. Here are some practical suggestions for making the most of those practices.

MAKING THE MOST OF THE PRACTICES OF WORSHIP

1. *Praise.* Whether you are singing one of the Psalms or a four-hundred-year-old hymn or a song written the week before, make it your intention to publish the truth of the words you are singing. Whether your voice is sweet or coarse, let it be your instrument of declaration. Sing it to God; sing it to the world. Praise is an act of spiritual assertion. The whole creation is shouting praise: "The heavens declare the glory of God; the skies proclaim the work of his hands. Day after day they pour forth speech; night after night they display knowledge.... Their voice goes out into all the earth, their words to the ends of the world" (Ps. 19:1–4). Human beings only need to be as smart as nature itself to know they must praise.

2. *Prayer.* When someone leads the congregation in prayer, don't think about what is being said to you. Make the words your own prayer to God. Use other quiet moments in worship to say your own silent prayers to God, making the whole worship service a running act of devotion.

3. *The public reading of Scripture.* Why did Paul tell the church leader Timothy "Devote yourself to the public reading of Scripture, to preaching and to teaching" (1 Tim. 4:13)? It was because Scripture is fully and truly the living Word of God. When the seed of that Word lands in soil that is rich and ready to receive it, a vivifying process is set in motion. We may not realize it immediately, but the sprouts of God's eternal truth will push up through the hard clay of our lives.

4. *Teaching and preaching.* This is to be a faithful elucidation of what is discovered in the Word of God. We need a rediscovery of and a recommitment to faith in the truth of the Word of God, as happened in the days of Ezra and Nehemiah when, on one day, all the people of God stood for hours to hear Scripture read and taught ("They read from the Book of the Law of God, making it clear and giving the meaning so that the people could understand what was being read" [Neh.

8:8]). If our goal in teaching and preaching is to inspire worship, then the clear aim is not to use words to explain our ideas but to use words to explain the Word.

5. *Offering.* When people rediscovered worship in King Hezekiah's day, the offerings flowed into heaps for four months, and storehouses for the offerings had to be built. Jesus stood by the temple and dignified the meager two-penny offering of a widow who offered all she had. Paul urged a church to make sure they excelled in "the grace of giving." If we make offering a pattern of worship, our disposition in life will keep soft and open instead of hardened and closed to a world of need around us. Offering is a continual repetition of the truth that we hold our resources as a stewardship instead of as a treasury. At death we will relinquish all. Offering gives us the joy in this life of seeing the effects of intentional relinquishment.

6. *Communion.* When Jesus said, "Do this in remembrance of me," he gave his followers a pattern for life. The moments of participating with Christ in communion (see 1 Cor. 10:16) should impress deeply on us the reality of sin, sacrifice, forgiveness, and Christ, who is the bread of life.

Whatever we do in worship, we do so in the name of Jesus because he is the one who fills the chasm. No one else can.

FOR PERSONAL REFLECTION

1. What does Psalm 145 say about worship?
2. Think through each of the practices of worship, identifying times when each practice played an influential role in your life.
3. What has to happen in a public worship service for God to be able to say, "I was worshiped"?

BELONGING

22

There are three things that made a deep impression on me the first time I rode in a jet airliner. One was the relentless acceleration of the takeoff, which was like a large invisible hand pressing me back in my seat. The second was the moment every vibration from the runway suddenly stopped as the wheels lifted off the ground and that driving machine instantaneously became a flying machine. The third—and this has to be an almost universal reaction—was the view of the landscape that presented itself as we quickly climbed. The farmland west of Chicago soon appeared as a patchwork of dark and light browns and greens and yellows as fine as if it were a quilt laid carefully across the land as far as the eye could see. Here was a macro pattern, shaped by human beings in neat forty- or eighty-acre plots and by the natural contours of rivers and streams and hills.

WHAT IS YOUR PATCHWORK?

Our relationships with others are a patchwork built up over years. We each fit in there somewhere, one patch surrounded by dozens of others and part of the whole picture. The pattern of our patch is one of the ways we are defined. You may say, "I'm a Minnesotan, a Lutheran, a Johnson, and a Swede," and in doing so you are describing part of who you are by identifying where you fit in the patchwork of the world—where you belong.

But then there is the ever-changing dynamic of relationships. Your ethnicity won't change, but your connections or disconnections with other human beings are constantly changing. These are the patterns that need to be developed; bad ones need to be avoided and good ones fostered.

What words would you use to describe the general shape of your relationships with other people: sporadic, deep, shallow, slim, stormy, stable, broad, narrow, shattered, wholesome?

The Bible makes it very clear, and experience bears it out, that God longs for us to have a quality of relationship with him and with others that is summarized in one potent word: *fellowship.* Now if this word is very familiar to you, it may bring to mind the sights and smells of steaming coffee, moist cake, and someone's living room or, in a church, a big tiled area called the fellowship hall. But fellowship is much more than friendly conversation conducted in a churchy kind of way.

LIVING AND LIFE-GIVING *KOINONIA*

"Fellowship" is the translation of the New Testament word *koinonia,* which means life held in common: a sharing, an association, a communion, a partnership. It is the mystery of the shared life, the surprising connection that binds people together. Fellowship is an intentional coming together, a purposeful commonality. It is a life-transforming, dynamic interaction between spiritual beings— that's you and me—and with God the Father, the Son, and the Holy Spirit, who are themselves a kind of divine fellowship and who make this supernatural connection possible between us.

Koinonia begins as a living connection with God. First John 1 begins with this stirring statement: "That which was from the beginning, which we have heard, which we have seen with our eyes, which we have looked at and our hands have touched—this we proclaim concerning the Word of life." (John is talking about his communion with Jesus.) And then John says, "We proclaim to you what we have seen and heard, so that you also may have fellowship with us. And our fellowship is with the Father and with his Son, Jesus Christ." The mystery of the shared life begins with this vital connection with Christ, then flows out into other relationships. But there is a caveat. "If we claim to have fellowship with him yet walk in the darkness, we lie and do not live by the truth. But if we walk in the light, as he is in the light, we have fellowship with one another, and the blood of Jesus, his Son, purifies us from all sin" (1 John 1:6).

God created us with a longing to belong. It is an unremitting desire to know how we fit into the vast patchwork that is the world we live in. Some feel blessed to belong to the family their blood comes from, others not. Some have a sense of identity with their nation, others have no such intuition. Some have a strong commitment to their favorite club or association and gladly follow the standards and attend the meetings that allow them to say, "I know I belong." But there is nothing that can compare with an abiding sense that one belongs to God and, as a consequence, belongs to the family of God. Far beyond just belonging to a church, this is the sense of coming home, of being home, of fitting into that great patchwork that is the way God created human beings to be.

THE BIRTH AND GROWTH OF FELLOWSHIP

Fellowship is a reality that, like other spiritual patterns, develops over a long period of time when we repeat obedient acts of connection. Sometimes there is immediate satisfaction, oftentimes not. (That's why obedience is important.) But if you believe in and commit to a pattern of *koinonia,* if you again and again approach and engage others whom God has defined as our brothers and sisters— spending time talking with them, working alongside them, praying for them and letting them pray for you, worshiping with them, going to their homes and allowing them into yours, learning their children's names and going to their parents' funerals, sending cards when they are ill, calling them when you've not seen them for a long time—you will be living the best kind of life that can be lived: the shared life.

Fellowship is a kind of spiritual friendship. Now think about how ordinary friendships develop. They don't happen suddenly. There are at least three phases to the birth of a friendship. First, some circumstance puts you together with another person; then you discover that you have some things in common or that you share interests; and then you spend more time with that other person; and gradually you come to the point where you say in your heart, "This is more than an acquaintance, more than an association—this is a friend."

So also, *koinonia* begins with circumstances of contact: worshiping next to someone, folding chairs with someone for a church dinner, traveling in a van to go do prison visitation with someone, sitting in someone's living room every Wednesday evening for a Bible study, being part of a prayer group with someone. From circumstance you go on to discovered interests, primarily God and the kingdom of God. You marvel together about how God has worked in impossible situations and discover together how to throw yourself on the mercy of God when circumstances leave you no other options. Then you spend time retracing the steps of your shared development. You see these people when they are at their best and when they are at their worst. And if you stick with them, not only when you get something from them but also when they get something from you, you will realize one day, "This is where I belong. I do fit into the patchwork of God's landscape. I have a family not based on my blood but on the blood of Jesus. I have friends whose common focus is not football but the kingdom of God."

THE UPS AND DOWNS OF FINDING SPIRITUAL FAMILY AND FRIENDS

Now let's be honest about the difficulties of forging spiritual friendships and finding a place in a spiritual family. To find *koinonia* is an unmatchable blessing, but it means joining with people who are profoundly imperfect. People can heal, but they can also hurt.

Fellowship friendships are encouraging, but they can also be a drain. But then, so are we all.

The alternative is simply unthinkable. Spiritual isolation means spiritual dissolution. Not to belong means wandering in a spiritual wasteland.

Small group fellowship is one of the best forms for experiencing *koinonia* and is enjoying a resurgence today, although this pattern goes back to the New Testament church. It was also one of the key features in the nation-changing revival of John Wesley's day, of German pietist groups, and others.

In the last thirty years I have experienced four different periods when I have participated in a home-based small group. I can say without hesitation that they have been some of the most important spiritual growth experiences of my life. The first group was a Bible study that I went to every Friday night while I was still in high school. The fifteen or twenty people who gathered in Dan and Bev's living room ranged from age seventeen to seventy. Every person who came was greeted at the door by the howling and barking of Maggie the beagle.

First there was a good cup of coffee, not in Styrofoam cups, but in real china or ceramic mugs. Of course there was cake too, usually the household favorite of the person providing refreshments that week. And after a couple of years, people began requesting their favorites. This was the time to say hello and to catch up on the casual details of our lives. Pure chitchat. Everybody held back the really important things, however, so that they could raise them as a matter of prayer later in the evening. Dan's living room was very long, which made for a great oval-shaped group of couches and chairs and pillows on the floor. Sitting near the woodstove was a good idea in cold months because it was the early 1970s and the U.S. was in the midst of an energy crisis.

There were three simple parts to the meeting itself. A few songs were offered in worship, *a cappella* or accompanied by a guitar. The sound was not impressive, perhaps just a step better than the typical sound of the happy birthday song at a party. But that of course didn't matter. What mattered is that twenty people who otherwise held virtually nothing in common were coming together in a moment of adoration of Father, Son, and Holy Spirit.

The second part of the meeting was the Bible study. Now the way we did our Bible study went against all of the rules of what we usually teach about the study of Scripture. Because all we did, really, was take a section of a biblical book, read three or four or five verses at a time, and then talk about the questions that arose in our minds and the applications that we could see for ourselves. The leader would gently nudge the discussion along, and when about an hour had passed, we closed our Bibles, and that was it. It was a little study and a lot of application. But I wouldn't trade that experience for anything, because for the three or four years that I was in this group, I experienced the living power of the Word of God. Everyone in that room would have said the same thing.

The third part of the meeting was prayer on behalf of each other. It was the first place I learned about my own hesitation to reveal my needs and shortcomings, but I also learned about the strength you receive when you do take the risk and let others pray for you. I learned much from listening to how veteran believers prayed for each other, how their prayers roamed and probed all possible points of connection between God's power and human need. And how could one be blessed more than to know that somebody in the group was going to be praying for you in the intervening week?

Another group that I joined was a brand-new thing that Elmbrook Church started in the mid-1970s called Neighborhood Groups. I was a college student at the time, and I heard that the church wanted all of us to gather in people's homes for a weeknight meeting of Bible study and prayer, and so I went. I was not faithful in attendance. But whenever I was there, once again I sensed the rightness and the health of meeting for the purpose of studying the Bible and praying together and getting to know the real concerns in each other's lives. This was also a time when Elmbrook Church was getting larger, and it became important to have a form of ministry where people would not slip through the cracks—where everyone would be in a group that knew when you were doing well, when you were hurting, and when you were getting out of line spiritually. It worked in the mid-70s, and it's been working ever since—that is, of course, for those who take the step to find fellowship.

When I returned to Elmbrook after seminary, my wife and I joined another Neighborhood Group. John and Shirley were the hosts. They lived a mile away from our house on Saylesville Road. Same agenda: friendly conversation, Bible study, worship, prayer. That group had a number of people who moved a lot. And of course, our group was the moving company. We got it down to an art. John usually organized the vehicles, I liked packing the trucks, and if the movees were not completely packed on the Saturday morning we arrived, we'd all join in ranting and raving.

A fourth experience of fellowship that I will always cherish is a group that was formed about thirteen years ago. We decided to meet every other Sunday evening, and less often in the summer months, frequently enough so that we could keep in contact, but less than a regular weekly meeting so that we would keep regular with it.

Over those thirteen years we have shared together the process of children growing up. We've prayed many hours for the challenges, opportunities, and difficulties in our kids' lives. We've been able to pray for each other when medical needs arose. Sometimes we confronted each other. Sometimes the larger group impressed on one person a strong piece of collective wisdom.

I vividly remember getting a phone call one morning three years ago, several weeks after I had my bicycle accident, and when I heard Bob say the words "Our group has been talking about your situation," I stiffened, because I knew what the next words were going to be: "We all know how much you've been looking forward to that camping trip out in Yellowstone, but we are concerned. We really wonder if you're in good enough shape to do it." I knew it. I knew it. I didn't want to change my plans. To be honest (which I didn't want to be), I knew that it was medically questionable whether we should drive all that way. But when I got that phone call, the formidable force of collective wisdom was coming my way. They weren't telling me what to do, but they were admonishing me—giving me a perspective I couldn't have. But they were right; I was wrong; my family was relieved. We waited a year and headed west the following summer.

I talk about these examples not as a way of saying that this is the way fellowship always happens but as one more testimony of the blessings of fellowship. If you have a small number of people in your life that you are getting to know better and better as sisters and brothers, and they are getting to know you better and better, it will bless you. It will be a powerful way God works his grace into your life.

The following prayer may set our hearts in the right direction, toward fellowship.

PRAY THIS

Dear God, I know I cannot live with spiritual loneliness. I know you speak through your Word, and you make your presence known in so many other ways. But I know I need other people. Help me to find my place in the landscape of your kingdom. Help me to get over the disappointments and hurts from the past. Grant me a greater desire to give than to get. Grant me the blessing of spiritual friendships. I cherish fellowship with you; help me to cherish fellowship with others. Please do what needs to be done so you will look at your family and smile. In Christ's name, Amen.

FOR PERSONAL REFLECTION

1. What are some situations in your life when fellowship has worked well and when it hasn't?
2. What are some of the most effective ways that people can join with each other in fellowship?
3. What is the role of suffering and adversity in forging friendships?
4. What does this phrase from 1 John 3 mean to you: "Our fellowship is with the Father and with his Son, Jesus Christ"?

THE ART
OF IMITATION

23

I saw a television news special the other day about paratroopers—not a calling for cowards. A paratrooper's amazing proficiency is developed only with rigorous drills in ever-increasing levels of difficulty. I learned that of all of the skills necessary to succeed as a paratrooper it all boils down to one decisive moment: hitting the ground and dropping safely. Ideally, five points should make contact with the ground: feet, calf, hip, side, shoulder, in one smooth motion (as smoothly, anyway, as a body slamming into the ground can be). There is only one way to acquire such a skill, only one way to have the confidence to drop thousands of feet onto hard ground. Over and over the trainees watch their instructors and mimic every move of every muscle. The trainees trust the expertise of their mentors, knowing that hundreds of times they have jumped out of planes, fallen through the sky, hit the ground, rolled, and picked themselves up—and lived to tell about it.

WATCHING THE WISER

We gain many abilities through the art of imitation. Learning to cook, to golf, to make cabinetry, to drive a car, to dance, to fly a plane, or to deliver a speech—all involve scrutinizing someone wiser and more experienced and then trying to do it the same way.

Should it come as a surprise to us that learning to live a quality spiritual life involves imitation too? Something in us resists that notion. Perhaps we believe that characteristics like being truthful, loving, patient, or fair-minded come directly from God. Imitation is one thing when you're learning golf, but can it possibly be one of the ways we learn to love?

The Bible teaches that God passes on to us spiritual strength, skills, and character through many means, and one of these means is, in fact, imitation. God oftentimes gives us truth in principle, but he also gives us truth by example: real, flesh-and-blood people who are walking illustrations of the spiritual lesson of the day.

The apostle Paul wrote to his beloved Christian friends in the city of Philippi and told them—as clearly as a paratroop drill instructor tells his recruits—to imitate those who are wiser and more experienced. "Join with others in following my example, brothers, and take note of those who live according to the pattern we gave you" (Phil. 3:17).

INTENTIONAL IMITATION

We have to swallow a lot of pride to learn by imitation. We want to be originals. Imitation may seem like mimicry, but parroting or mimicking is mindless copying. Imitation is thoughtful and purposeful training, which is what it means to be a disciple.

Imitation is almost inevitable. Children grow up imitating their parents (often unconsciously) in how they speak to others, how they spend money, how they handle frustrations, how they work out conflicts. Often a parent's attitudes toward ethnic groups, their political sentiments, and their spiritual assumptions are gradually imprinted on a child's character.

It is just as easy to imitate bad values and lifestyles as good ones, of course. That is why we must be intentional about the examples we follow. Third John 11 says, "Dear friend, do not imitate what is evil but what is good."

When Paul says we should note those who "live according to the pattern we gave you," he means that we should note both their habits and their character. Any devotion pattern and any character pattern can be learned, in some fashion, through imitation.

When we see examples of people who are much more patient than we are, or who have uninhibited joy, or who seem like they are graduate students in prayer while we are in the elementary grades, we could just get discouraged. But that, surely, is the last thing God wants to happen to us. God has given us permission to be called disciples. And a disciple is a learner. To say "I am a disciple of Jesus" is to say "I know I have so much to learn, so far to go. I'm just glad this Master has accepted me into his school."

We need to keep our eyes open so that when we spot people who display godly patterns of character and habit, we can learn from them. Imitation is a lifestyle of watching, studying, and applying— always, of course, with God's guidance.

HOW DO YOU DO THAT?

If you respect someone who displays steady patience, ask him, "Just how do you do that?" When you are blessed by a thoughtful and loving note sent by someone, ask yourself, "Is there someone I could send a note to in the next two or three days?" If you know someone who is faithful and trustworthy to other people, try to understand where that faithfulness comes from. When a friend displays self-control in tempting circumstances, learn how that person has learned to step carefully through the minefield of enticement.

We learn to pray by picking up many small examples from a wide variety of people. We would do well to continually learn from others how they read Scripture in ways that allow what they read to shape their lives.

Today the art of imitation is sometimes called "discipling" or "mentoring." If a particular person is in some unique way a model or mentor for you, consider that a blessing. But keep in mind that most people are mentored in little ways by numerous people. None of us should be true disciples of anybody but Jesus himself.

As we search for examples or mentors, we are not limited to people we know. We can imitate people we have never met, people who live far away, even people who live in a different century. You may be so familiar with a couple of your favorite authors that they seem almost like friends. There is no reason you cannot consider them your mentors.

IMITATE FAITH

Above all others, faith is the one character quality we should strive to imitate. If we do this, many other issues fall into place. Hebrews 13:7 says, "Remember your leaders, who spoke the word of God to you. Consider the outcome of their way of life and imitate their faith." Imitate *faith*. Why is that so important? Because faith is the passageway through which the life-changing grace and power of God enters our lives. Faith in Christ is the engine of love, the wellspring of joy, the foundation of peace. Faith in Christ causes us to loosen our grip so that we can be patient, kind, and gentle. Faith links us to the power of God so that we can have self-control by being under his control. Faith opens our eyes to God's own goodness and makes us long for his goodness to fill us. Imitate faith. The most important thing other believers can teach us is how to believe.

Thankfully, we are not called to go looking for people who wear spiritual accomplishments like medals on their chests. Rather, when we find people who walk by faith in good times and bad—when they are doing well and when they have failed—people who go long to find the grace of God in the day that lies ahead, then we know we've found people whom God can use as models.

FOR PERSONAL REFLECTION

1. Who are a few people you believe you would like to imitate, and in what specific ways?

2. What kinds of models would you find especially helpful to you at this time in your life (for example, models of faith, hope, love, joy, peace, patience, kindness, goodness, gentleness, faithfulness, self-control, prayer, Scripture reading, or meditation)?

3. How do you handle the disappointment of discovering that someone you looked up to is a fallible human being?

ALONE, BUT NOT LONELY

24

Some time ago the radio in the car I usually drive went dead. For a week this was a nuisance. Then I began to enjoy the lack of chatter and music and advertisments. I could spend fifteen minutes here and there in my day not being carried along by the raging river of information from news radio. The quiet times in my small sedan came to be some of my favorite times to think and pray. And though my kids complain when they have to ride with me in this silent vehicle, I just haven't gotten around to getting that sound system repaired yet (though I'm pretty sure it's just a blown fuse). It's been about three years now.

Now I can't say that this represents the best example of solitude, which allows us to have clear and concentrated time alone with God. But it strikes me that it is so difficult to find some silence in the modern world that a car ride without radio seems important.

SWEET SOLITUDE

The word *solitude* (whose Latin root, *solus*, means "alone") sounds attractive to some people and to others sounds like torture. There is a town in the Rocky Mountains named Solitude. Where else but in Utah would you find a town by that name? Does that sound appealing to you? Now there is a ski resort there, near the top of Big Cottonwood Canyon. People go there to be removed, to draw away, to disengage their gears from the normal machinery of their lives.

Many of us live with the contradiction of wanting to disengage, to run to a simpler place where we can shut out the din and gain something in our knowledge of God, but finding it difficult to stay in these quiet places. We live with the tension of needing to be alone with God but feeling exposed and unprotected when we're not surrounded by the ordinary people and furniture and contraptions of our lives. But this remains true: "[There is] a time to be silent and a time to speak" (Eccl. 3:7).

We should not think that solitude is an issue just for a peculiar subset of believers—those who occasionally think they would like to be monks (if they weren't married, or if they weren't investment bankers, or if they didn't like football so much). Solitude is a gift and a challenge for every believer, because it is simply the commitment to having segments of time when we seek to be with God and God alone. *Solus* means aloneness, not loneliness. In fact, when we are alone with God we have some of the best opportunities to access the fullness of Christ. Sometimes the best way to get filled is to get the clutter out of the way. Times of solitude are like remodeling a room in your house. Clear it out, look at the blank walls, contemplate what really belongs there, and then deliberately place what you have decided needs to be in the room.

JESUS WITHDREW

Solitude is a pattern for every believer because it was a conspicuous habit in the life of Jesus. "Jesus *often* withdrew to lonely places and prayed" (Luke 5:16, emphasis added).

Those "lonely places" were the wilderness, the deserted places. One translation says Jesus "would often slip away."

Note that Jesus did this often. He did it to pray. He did it when he was busiest, doing the most fantastic work. Luke tells us that after healing a man with leprosy, reports about his power spread quickly, and vast crowds sought him out to hear him preach and to be healed of their diseases. Just when things were getting interesting, Jesus headed for the wilderness. He apparently had not heard aphorisms like "Strike while the iron's hot," "Make hay while the sun shines," or "Seize the day." Rather, he did in each day what was right for that day.

This is not a picture of Jesus taking a much-needed vacation from an intense career. Rather, it is a pattern of alternating between life together and life alone. You may want to stop and assess where you are right now in your life. Is it all life together (and so you need some solitude) or all life alone (and so you need to seek some fellowship)?

The Gospels tell us that Jesus went to places of solitude under many different circumstances—sometimes after a taxing time, sometimes before an important turning point, and sometimes because it simply was time.

WHERE DO YOU FIND SOLITUDE IN THE TWENTY-FIRST CENTURY?

What does a devotion pattern of solitude look like for us in the twenty-first century?

Solitude can be . . .

- A quiet time in the morning when you avoid everyone else in the household so that you can speak with God and ask him to speak with you.
- Taking half a day or a whole day by yourself away from home and all your normal concerns and responsibilities to let some really important spiritual issues rise to the top level of your mind and heart.
- Spending one hour after you've finished reading an important book or section of the Bible to meditate on what you have learned.
- Driving in the car without the sound of the radio, a CD, or a cassette, sorting through some of the spiritual concerns of your life.

- Taking a walk along the shore or in the woods and asking God to give you a perspective on your place in his creation.
- Spending ten minutes in a quiet time when you neither read nor pray but simply ask God to bring his thoughts to you.
- Taking an annual or semiannual day retreat at some quiet place with a plan for reading, praying, resting, and writing.

As I write this I'm sitting alone, very alone, in a small library at a Christian retreat center. I wish I could say that I am here because I had the personal discipline to step away from my normal setting to think, pray, and write. But the truth is, my wife kicked me out of the house. Oh, it wasn't mean-spirited or anything. She knew just a bit better than I did that I needed the break and that I needed to finish this manuscript. She also knew that the best way for this to happen was for me to spend five days away from the house and the office, to work in the prayerful wooded setting of this center. So I heard her calling the center on Sunday night, asking if there was a room for one more procrastinating pastor, and next thing I knew I was halfway through a wonderful stay with no television, no radio, no Internet hookup. And I've taken in the hours of quietness and prayerful walks in the woods and have gotten a few thousand more words written.

THE REWARD BEHIND THE CLOSED DOOR

Solitude is not seeking God out of nothingness. Silence itself has no voice. It is not the Eastern idea of enlightenment through negation. Aloneness with God is a stepping aside or, as the Gospels say, withdrawing to a deserted place, slipping away from the crowds for a higher purpose. It is why Jesus said, "But when you pray, go into your room, close the door and pray to your Father, who is unseen. Then your Father, who sees what is done in secret, will reward you" (Matt. 6:6). This is in contrast to showy people who want everyone to see their spiritual fervor displayed on the street corner. Jesus said spiritual show-offs "will be punished most severely" (Luke 20:47). One thing is for sure: no public applause comes from solitude.

There are many barriers to being *solus* with God, which is why it does not come easy for most of us. We may long for solitude, but it is not easy to be alone, spiritually naked as it were, before God. Often an internal voice says, "You're not being very productive right now," or "You've got better things to do than this," or "So and so is waiting for you, God will always be there," or "Who are you to think you have the luxury of stepping away?" We may be embarrassed at how easily our minds wander or bounce around. Being *solus* with God turns into ordinary daydreaming, so we just give up.

Another barrier to solitude is the fact that no one will criticize us for *not* spending time alone with God. After all, who knows? Who is keeping track? Who wouldn't much rather have you doing something for them? Slipping away to the wilderness doesn't usually raise our stature in other people's minds.

Yet consider this: What would we like better than to see someone we know have times when he or she can step aside, get spiritually rested and recharged, and come back with more of the life of God to share—or even a greater burden if that is appropriate? If this is something we would wish for someone else, why not allow it for ourselves?

FOR PERSONAL REFLECTION

1. What positive experiences have you had with being alone with God?

2. What have you discovered are good ways to make this happen in your life?

3. What are some of the barriers you face?

4. How would you structure a whole day focusing on meditation and prayer? Where would you go? When *will* you go?

FULLNESS AND THE EXPENDED LIFE

25

A couple of months ago I spent several hours walking around the great city of Beijing, China, where I was participating in a conference. The phrase "sea of humanity" has become a cliché, but in China such clichés are the perfect description. I stood for a while in the middle of Tiananmen Square, which I am told is the largest square in the world. Massive government buildings and historic buildings border it on all sides, but in the square itself was a steady stream of humanity, some moving north, south, east, or west, others cutting across at an angle, some, like me, meandering a bit trying to decide which way to go, changing course a few times along the way. My lemon-yellow jacket made me feel far too conspicuous, like a big bumblebee in a vast gray field. But most people were oblivious to the others moving through the square, including the soldiers who march in groups of six or eight in the straightest lines possible. I wonder what an aerial view of it all would look like. What would someone make of the patterns of the paths chosen by so many different people, going so many different places?

BEING EMPTIED TO BE FILLED

Most people want their lives to have some kind of meaningful path, to know that the course they are setting is getting them somewhere. One of our basic instincts is to believe that the path to a content and full life is to fill it with things. Acquisitiveness is sometimes the only instinct people go on, because nobody has ever pointed out an alternative path.

Jesus did give us an alternative when he said, "It is more blessed to give than to receive." This is not just a nice sentiment but a revolutionary call and a great paradoxical mystery.

So many of the most important truths in life are paradoxes—two propositions that appear to contradict each other—but the truth is found in the tension between the two.

What does it take to have a God-filled life? Here's one paradox: If you want to have a full life, you must empty it. To put it another way, emptying leads to filling. This is the biblical idea of service, and it is one of the most formative habits anyone can experience. Think about it. Do you know many hoarders who have a sense of freedom in their lives, who have lightness in their step and joy about facing the next day? Then think about people you know who are real givers. They expend themselves on others. They lightly hold their time, their money, and their energy—not because they are careless but because they are in control by being free to be generous.

Jesus said, "No one can serve two masters. Either he will hate the one and love the other, or he will be devoted to the one and despise the other. You cannot serve both God and Money" (Matt. 6:24). This is the kind of passage that stings, but let's not miss the focus of it. This is a manifesto about service. Step one: Serve God or serve an idol. Simple (but difficult) choice. Next step: What does it mean, exactly, to serve God? One way is worship. As we saw in an earlier chapter, one of the main words for worship in the New Testament is also translated as "service." You worship and you serve; you serve and you worship. The common denominator is that you are giving.

That is why Jesus told Peter three times that if he really loved Jesus, Peter would serve (feed, tend) Jesus' sheep. Jesus was saying,

"If you love me, you must love those whom I love." He was also implying that one of his chosen means of pouring out his grace on the people of this world in thousands of different ways would be through his followers.

WHAT DOES EVERYDAY SERVICE LOOK LIKE?

What does a pattern of service look like? For starters, let's take the ways we can make a difference in the local church we attend. Service may be:

- greeting people at the door
- administrating a program
- singing with a group that goes to a nursing home
- teaching children
- setting up chairs for meetings
- teaching a Bible study
- chairing a committee
- praying for leaders
- visiting the ill
- directing traffic in the parking lot
- counting the offering
- selling tickets for a concert
- escorting newcomers to classes
- sewing costumes for an Easter play
- cooking meals for shut-ins
- organizing the church library
- assisting with mailings
- writing to missionaries
- sponsoring a refugee family
- editing a newsletter for a ministry
- being a counselor at a youth camp
- visiting people in prison

And these are just opportunities to serve in the church. The great thing about the discipline of service is that opportunities to serve can be found, to the glory of Christ and to the growth of our spiritual lives, almost anywhere we are around other people. Service should become an instinct that is the shape of the whole way we relate to others. It is holding the door open for someone, showing more interest in others than in talking about yourself, spending your valuable time and energy to help someone out, giving to the poor. A *diakonos* (the New Testament word for "servant") is someone waiting to be called into God's service, whether in a small way or a costly way.

FINDING THE MOTIVATION, ANSWERING THE CALL

Where does the motivation come from when we just don't feel like giving (which, for most of us will be most of the time)?

Jesus told us, "If you give someone a drink of water, you're giving it to me; visit someone in prison, you're visiting me; give someone something to wear, and you're clothing me; take care of someone who is ill, and you're caring for me." Can it possibly be that simple? That direct? Jesus said this kind of thing again and again. And when he bent down to wash his disciples' feet and dry them with a towel, he simply said, "Now I want you to do this for each other." This is the universal and enduring call to service. A true follower of Jesus takes pleasure in assuming the fundamental role of being a servant of God. Martin Luther called this true freedom. In his *The Freedom of a Christian*, Luther made this landmark statement: "A Christian is a perfectly free lord of all, subject to none. A Christian is a perfectly dutiful servant of all, subject to all." We have complete spiritual freedom in Christ, and the highest possible use of that freedom is to serve others.

Ephesians 4:12 says that God has given his many gifts to the church to "prepare God's people for works of service." If you belong to the church, then realize that you have not signed up for membership in a club or a mutual interest association but have joined in a radical mission to engage every member of the church in the life-giving expenditure of sweat and tears in response to Christ.

Emptying does lead to filling. But we won't gain unless we choose to lose.

Someone once gave me such a riveting illustration of this idea that I repeat it often. There are two main bodies of water in Israel: the Sea of Galilee and the Dead Sea. These two bodies of water are in a direct north-south line along the Great Rift Valley and are connected by the Jordan River. Clear, fresh water from underground springs flows into the Sea of Galilee, which in turn gives up some of itself by flowing south into the Jordan. Galilee is a beautiful, active lake full of life, which has sustained fishermen in the region for millennia. The Dead Sea, by contrast, is a shallow, selfish basin that has no outlet and thus hoards the water that flows into it. Water evaporates, leaving behind brackish, clouded water so dense that if you swim in it, you will bob like a cork. But the Dead Sea sustains no life and no one.

"It is more blessed to give than to receive." This is a matter of spiritual life or spiritual death.

The Sea of Galilee receives every day and gives every day. If the matter of spiritual life or spiritual death is a simple as that, why is it so hard for us to let the grace of God flow in and flow out? I can think of several reasons.

First, serving can be hard work. Nobody needs our small tokens of service; they need real service. This may mean spending many hours with someone, and you may or may not be appreciated for what you do.

Second, serving is others-focused, not self-focused. This cuts against our nature. But that is why service is therapeutic (healing) for us. We don't always know when we are stuck in self-absorption. We need the pool of Narcissus to be stirred up so that we get our focus off ourselves and onto the vast needy world around us and the formidable movement of God in this world.

"The Son of Man did not come to be served, but to serve, and to give his life as a ransom for many" (Mark 10:45). Therefore, if we are to be formed into the image of Christ, we must ask God to make servanthood a pattern as habitual as anything in our lives.

PRAY THIS

Dear God, help me to believe that to serve you by serving others is the only way for me to be spiritually alive. Grant me the assurance that if I give, I will not lose anything but what I should perhaps lose anyway. Forgive me for hesitation, for selfishness, and for lack of faith. Help me to be proud to be your servant but never to be proud because of my effort. Open my eyes today to the ways I can be your humble servant. In Jesus' name, Amen.

FOR PERSONAL REFLECTION

1. Whom do you know who serves with a good attitude and (as far as you know) the right motives? How do they get past the barriers of selfishness and keep on giving with joy?

2. What are the barriers to our being servants of Christ?

3. How do you deal with disappointment when your best intentions to serve don't turn out well?

4. If Jesus were physically beside you for the next few days, coaching you along the way, where would he tell you to serve in small ways and large ways?

ALL OF GRACE

In our search for a God-filled life, we have looked at the shape and substance of that life (the character patterns of love, joy, peace, patience, kindness, goodness, gentleness, faithfulness, and self-control), and we have looked at the devotion patterns that draw us closer to God. From the beginning to the end of our search, we must focus on one all-important dynamic: the God-filled life is filled *by God*. It is all of grace—or it is just a play on a stage.

Whenever I've driven up the winding road of a high mountain pass that snakes between the edge of the rock and a sheer drop, I've noticed my knuckles getting a little whiter, my palms a little sweatier, my foot lighter on the accelerator, and my eyes ever more vigilant for the white line that marks the outer edge of the lane. And I'm always so glad for those guardrails placed where the danger of slipping off into catastrophe is the greatest.

Keeping in the lane has been one of my greatest concerns since I started writing on the theme of developing a God-filled life. As we talk about Christian character and a lifestyle of devotion, we are driving through a marvelous landscape, but one that requires us to navigate tricky curves on the edge of a cliff. What I am talking about is the solidity and the weight of the glory of God on the one side (the mountain) and the cliff of self-confidence or self-reliance on the other.

My knuckles get white writing about these themes because it would be so easy to steer off the edge of the road into the open air of platitude and undue confidence. Spiritual life is not at its core about attainment; it is about relationship. God wants progress in our lives, for sure. But he wants progress because he wants us.

So let this be the last word and the guardrail that will keep us in the lane: it is all of grace.

GOD MUST DO WHAT ONLY GOD CAN DO

Grace is a true distinctive of Christian faith, and it is one reason why Christianity seems like an odd and inscrutable proposition to skeptics. Human nature tells us that we should be getting the job done ourselves—climb that mountain, plant your flag. But only God can do the work of transformation, and certainly only he can fill our lives.

There is mighty power in this soft-edged truth of divine charity. Christianity says that all that we are and all that we have comes straight from the beneficent heart of the Creator. This speaks volumes about the Creator and the creation. Furthermore, any good thing that comes into our life or any good thing we can accomplish is only because of the flow of God's grace through our lives. Where else could goodness come from? And how else could we be confident that living in the fullness of Christ is possible?

What is grace, in itself? Well, it doesn't stand by itself. We can only comprehend it as a characteristic of the personal God. Love does not exist in the abstract, and neither does grace. It is the inexorable force of the generosity of God. It is, if I could coin an awkward word, his givingness. This is who God is and what he does: he gives and gives and gives, not because he has to but because he chooses to. His givingness is not indiscriminate. Yes, God "causes his sun to rise on the evil and the good, and sends rain on the righteous and the unrighteous" (Matt. 5:45), but the full vigor of God's grace is seen in active covenant relationships. A God-filled life begins with God's own grace-filled covenant promise: "I will be their God and they will be my people."

Now this is why we should be interested in character patterns and devotion patterns. We are not building a tower to reach to heaven; that's already been tried. We are not able to do that, and so God doesn't allow it. Rather, we are coming to the mountain. Moses was transformed by the days he spent on Mount Sinai; a radiance still lingered on his face when he came back to the people. Jesus took Peter, James, and John up a mountain, where he was transfigured and they were transformed. And so we come to 2 Corinthians 3:18, which says, "We, who with unveiled faces all reflect the Lord's glory, are being transformed into his likeness with ever-increasing glory, which comes from the Lord, who is the Spirit."

All of grace.

Grace is forgiveness when we fail, mercy when we are out of line, strength when we are weary, protection when we put ourselves in danger, guidance when we are confused, long-suffering when we are insufferable. Grace is divine love surging from the immortal to the mortal.

The biblical idea of patterns for life is a thing of grace. God seems to be telling us, "I'm not directing you to perform heroic spiritual acts every day; I am inviting you to take one step at a time, begin a new habit, begin setting a new pulse, and these patterns will set your life in a direction toward me."

So when we say, "God please fill my life; please shape the character of my life; please develop healthy and holy habits in my life," we are saying, "God, please pour out the grace, abundant grace, for that is my only hope."

GRACE AT EVERY TURN

How important is it for us to focus on grace? The voice of Scripture is loud and clear: spiritual life itself is the result of a daily infusion of grace in every form.

Grace and truth came through Jesus (John 1:17). We are made right with God, freely by his grace (Rom. 3:24). Where sin is on the rise, grace rises all the more (Rom. 5:20). A right life is not attained by obeying a law but by living under God's grace (Rom. 6:14). By the grace of Jesus, he became poor though he was rich, so that through his poverty we might become rich (2 Cor. 8:9). God is able to make grace abound in our lives so that we have everything we need, and we will abound in every good work (2 Cor. 9:8). When we feel weak, that is when God's power is made perfect, because his grace is sufficient (2 Cor. 12:8). Forgiveness and redemption is rich grace lavished on us (Eph. 1:7–8). We can be strong in grace (2 Tim. 2:1) and can fill our conversations with grace (Col. 4:6). We will find grace in the time of need, and so we can approach God's throne of grace with confidence (Heb. 4:16). God gives grace to the humble (James 4:6). And God wants us to grow in the grace and knowledge of our Lord and Savior Jesus Christ (2 Peter 3:18).

Remember doubting Thomas? The man who missed seeing the resurrected Jesus claimed he would not believe unless he could see the marks from the nails in Jesus' hands. The word *mark* in John 20:25 is "pattern." When he did see the impressions of cruelty in goodness, the pattern of love that sacrifices, Thomas was ready to be shaped by that abundant grace for the rest of his life. And so must we.

So we end where we began, with a passionate prayer from the apostle Paul:

"And I pray that you, being rooted and established in love, may have power, together with all the saints, to grasp how wide and long and high and deep is the love of Christ, and to know this love that surpasses knowledge—that you may be filled to the measure of all the fullness of God" (Eph. 3:17–19).

And we may again make that prayer our own.

PRAY THIS

Lord, I pray that I would have roots as strong as those of a magnificent tree, going deeply into your love, and as strong as a building built on the foundation of your love. Please give me the ability to take in, to understand, to apply, and to own the reality of your love, which is wide enough to get around my whole life, long enough to last my whole life and beyond, high enough to elevate me to the stature you desire, and deep enough to fill the unseen pockets of decay and emptiness in the hidden parts of my life. Please fill my life and fulfill my life because I know—I know—I cannot do it on my own. Amen.

FOR PERSONAL REFLECTION

1. Recount some of the key times in your life when you have experienced the grace of God.

2. Which of the biblical passages quoted in this chapter is most striking to you at this time, and why?

3. What is your main prayer for the pattern of your life at this time?

We want to hear from you. Please send your comments about this book to us in care of zreview@zondervan.com. Thank you.

GRAND RAPIDS, MICHIGAN 49530 USA

WWW.ZONDERVAN.COM